Relating Redefined

Discovering the New "Language" for Communicating

John Narciso, Ph.D.
David Burkett, M.S.J.

Revised Edition
1994

Library of Congress Cataloging-in-Publication Data

Narciso, John (date)
Relating Redefined

1. Interpersonal relations. 2. Communications – Psychological Aspects. I.
Burkett, David (date) joint author. II. Title.

HM 132.N37   158".2
ISBN 1-879797-01-1 pbk.

Published in 1992, 1994 by Redman-Wright Publishing.

Published in 1986 by Prentice-Hall Press, A Division of Simon &
Schuster, Inc.

Originally published in 1975 by Prentice-Hall, Inc.

Distributed by:
Redman-Wright Publishing
14123 Fairway Oaks
San Antonio, Texas 78217-1648
Tel/Fax (210) 650-5763

Fifth Printing 1999

Relating Redefined

John Narciso, at the time this book was written, was Professor of Psychology and Director of the Counseling Center at Trinity University in San Antonio, Texas. He also maintained a private practice as a consulting psychologist.

David Burkett was Associate Professor of Communication at Trinity University and a former practicing journalist.

Subsequently, both have devoted their professional efforts to consulting with schools, business groups and government agencies.

Acknowledgments

Dorothy Vance, Cynthia Sanders and Dennis Narciso assisted in the preparation of this manuscript. We acknowledge their significant contribution to *Relating Redefined.*

Quotations from *The Second Sin,* by Thomas Szasz, are used by kind permission of Doubleday & Company, Inc., and McIntosh and Otis, Inc. Copyright 1973 by Thomas S. Szasz

Author's Note

This book was originally published in 1975 by Prentice-Hall Inc. under the title Declare Yourself. I have waited through sixteen years and sixteen printings to have the right to change the title which was determined by others under the publishing contract.

Originally intended as an antidote to the ME generation's *tell everybody all your feelings about everything,* the book was often perceived as quite the opposite because of its title.

The title Declare Yourself is a second person imperative! The text encourages first person expressions without demanding. Quite a difference.

As in the original, the focus in this revised edition is on understanding that while I am only in charge of ME directly, I am always in a context of the WE.

Presented here are some alternative ways the ME in the WE can behave to create a mutually productive relationship across the lives of both persons in a dyad.

The new title is an invitation to explore and develop additional skills in relating.

John Narciso
San Antonio, 1994

Contents

Are Feelings Caused by Something Outside?
Can Feelings be Shared?
Can Others be Responsible for My Feelings?

Relating Redefined

one

A Round Earth Theory

In San Antonio July afternoons are warm and humid. On this particular afternoon, two colleagues talk over coffee. Both were on the faculty of Trinity University. One was a professor of psychology and a practicing psychologist. John Narciso directed the university's counseling center and traveled the length of the nation talking with groups about interpersonal relationships.

The other was a journalist, a former newspaper reporter, magazine writer, radio newscaster, and public relations practitioner. David Burkett was a professor of journalism, teaching classes and directing workshops in interpersonal communication.

These two men had known one another for several years. More recently, their paths had come closer together as they developed and taught courses to help students make sense of themselves, their worlds, and all the other people who shared those worlds with them.

Both of them believed that *how* people *chose* to relate to one another was the key to interpersonal relationships.

1

They also believed that the basic function of learning was to change behavior.

On this day, they decided to write a short book, explaining some of the things that they taught about in their classes at Trinity. Their book was to concern how people choose from among their learned alternatives to relate to one another. Consider that.

Choosing How to Relate

A person is not born knowing how to behave with other people and what to think of them. He learns from his parents and other authority figures—teachers, aunts, uncles, grandparents, and the grownups next door. He* also learns from other youngsters—brothers, sisters, playmates up and down the street, the TV and the Internet.

Unless something happens that makes him question the procedures passed along to him, he probably relates in much the same way through adolescence and adulthood.

Evidence suggests that many of these ways of behaving may not be appropriate or worthwhile. The media talk about the increasing suicide rate, the excessive use of alcohol, and drugs being used to separate self from the real world. Ineffective relationships are reflected in the divorce rate, in crime, in the number of people who visit psychiatrists and psychologists, in the thousands of persons who make tranquilizers a steady diet, and in the scores of young people who spend their time drifting from place to place.

---

* To avoid vague references and awkward double pronouns, I will use third-person singular he. No sexism is intended.

The authors believe that the discontent so many people are experiencing may be the result of limited options and alternatives in the ways people behave interpersonally.

Learning New Options

Edward Bear in *Winnie The Pooh* (New York: Dell, a Yearling Book, 1954) also was discontented:

Here is Edward Bear, coming downstairs now, bump, bump, bump on the back of his head behind Christopher Robin. It is, as far as he knows, the only way of coming downstairs, but sometimes he feels that there really is another way, if only he could stop bumping for a moment and think of it.

Edward Bear was limited in the ways he had of coming down the stairway. Had he been able to learn more options, he might have chosen a more appropriate way. He would have had more freedom.

Young adults speak of freedom when they leave home to attend college. They appear to be in charge of themselves and would propose that they are free persons, able to relate to other people in the ways in which they choose.

Jeffrey Schrank, in *Teaching Human Beings* (Boston, Beacon Press, 1972), is perhaps more insightful in his description of the young adult. Schrank says that the young adult grows up learning that he is not important, that he needs permission to do things, that he is controlled by outside forces, and that he must hide his real self. He believes that learning is something given to him by other people and that he must become what others want him to become.

The young adult may be anything but free.

He may have learned too few options.

Hundreds of years ago, there were few options in how people perceived our earth. The common belief was that the earth was flat. Geography and other disciplines were built on that belief. People bumped along on the premise that if one traveled far enough, he would fall from the edges of the earth. Evidence seemed to support the premise.

One day, a daring person suggested that the earth might not be flat but round instead. Decades later, when explorers proved that indeed the world was a nearly round object, there were new alternatives in geography and the other disciplines.

In this book, the authors propose a new "Round Earth Theory" of interpersonal relationships in the hope that some flat earth assumptions will be challenged even though "present evidence" is readily accepted.

The authors propose that since people *learn* how to behave, they are capable of learning additional alternatives to the ways they now interact with other people.

The authors agree that their own lives, professionally and personally, have been affected greatly by the options they now present in this book. They have also witnessed remarkable changes in students, clients, managers, teachers, married couples, and others who have learned and practiced these alternatives.

The new options they propose invite a person to be more in charge of himself, to be more in control of his life. Beyond that, the options presented in this book may offer new Round Earth perspectives on the ways people traditionally view religion, psychology, mental illness and sickness. How each person responds to his world depends upon how he has learned to conceptualize it.

This book is written in the first person singular, as though one individual authored its pages, but it reflects two men and their thinking at a particular time. They invite the reader to make it a threesome, recognizing that whether the reader agrees or disagrees is not as important as is his exposure to these additional alternatives.

two

Words Are Not Realities

Think with me about the attributes or characteristics of what you consider to be a good relationship. The relationships may be between any two people—husband and wife, roommates, neighbors, friends, business associates, youngsters, children and their parents. You might find it helpful to jot some of these attributes in the margin of this book before you continue reading.

Important Personal Words

Through years of seminars and classes, I've asked hundreds of people to make a similar list. Predictably, many of the same words appear on those lists: *love, trust, consideration, tolerance, respect, sensitivity, forgiveness, communication.*

These are big words to most people. They become nearly sacred. We lock into them and commit ourselves to them. We say that people die for them, and many of us do that a little every day.

Not many years ago my list would have included many

of these words.

I was enormously concerned with being "loved" and "respected."

I was pleased when someone offered me "trust" and "consideration," and I certainly believed I needed to be "forgiven" occasionally.

The way I perceive these words has changed. This began to happen several years ago through my rereading of P.W. Bridgman, the Nobel Prize-winning physicist.

Operational Definitions

In 1959, two years before he died, Bridgman wrote *The Way Things Are* (Cambridge, Harvard University Press). In the Introduction, he talked of his "constant practice of 'operational analysis,'"the analysis of "doings or happenings" rather than of "static abstractions."

As far back as the 1920s, Bridgman was suggesting that since many words represented static abstractions, scientists should deal instead with operational definitions in reporting scientific events. *An operational definition describes an event or happening.* Bridgman maintained that an operational analysis was "a sort of analysis which everyone can learn to make" and that it "puts nearly everything in a different and a fresher light."

Imagine the year 1915. In a psychology laboratory a young man conducts an experiment involving white rats. He labels one variable "hunger." When he prepares his final project report, he will record that the rats were "hungry" as one of the experimental conditions.

Later, when other psychologists attempt to understand

that study or to replicate it, they will not know what actually took place in the experiment when they read the word "hungry." The word "hungry" is not an event or a happening, although it does represent an actual occurrence.

Since the 1920s, because of Bridgman and others who agreed with him, the scientific world has adopted operational terms in scientific writing. Today's psychologist would report not that the laboratory rats were "hungry," but rather that each "did not eat for eight hours" or sixteen hours or whatever the interval was. The psychologist could center on events. and happenings.

I understood this. I had authored scientific papers using operational definitions. I knew quite well that science editors would not accept papers written in nonoperational terms.

Now, as I was reintroduced to Bridgman through his final book, I was struck by the fact that operational definitions were not generally used in interpersonal relationships.

Words, I know, are not realities. They aren't tangible things, real items, substances to carry from one interpersonal relationship to another. They frequently do not describe actual behavior. Instead of using such abstractions as "love" and "trust," I could describe what was actually happening or what I wanted to happen. If I did that, I would be making my message clearer to another person.

I was fascinated by the idea.

I read Bridgman's next paragraph.

"Analyzing the world in terms of doings or happenings, as contrasted with analyzing in terms of things or static elements," he wrote, "amounts to doing something new and unusual. I believe that history shows that, whenever human beings find how to do something new, new vistas open."

From Labels to Behaviors

I was launched on a continuing expedition, an adventure which has changed my life and my relationships with other people considerably.

In a workshop soon after reading Bridgman, I asked that participants consider attributes of effective interpersonal relationships. One word that was suggested was the word "tolerance." Several of the participants said that they "believed" in "tolerance."

I pointed out that "tolerance" was not a thing to "believe in." "Tolerance" was just a word, an abstraction. It did not exist in the real world, but behavior does.

How could an observer know, I asked, that in a given situation there was "tolerance"? What would literally happen if two people were "tolerating"?

Two men came forward when I requested volunteers.

I asked them to demonstrate "tolerance."

After a few moments, one of the two said that "tolerance" was something that had to come over a period of time; it had to develop. I assured them that they could take all the time they needed.

Several minutes later, and after a rather animated conversation between the two men, they announced to the seminar that they were prepared to *demonstrate* "tolerance." As we watched, the two men approached each other, smiled, and shook hands.

"Do you shake hands with people you don't 'tolerate'"? I asked.

"Yes," they said, "sometimes."

I explained that I had seen no "tolerance." What I had seen was two men shaking hands. "Tolerance" is an abstraction; two men shaking hands is an actual event. It is operational, reality, a happening in the real world. Two men shaking hands is the description of a behavior that we all had experienced with our own eyes.

At another seminar, an elementary-school teacher said that he was having trouble with one of his students.

"Tim is defiant," the teacher said. "I never saw such a defiant kid."

"What does Tim do?" I asked.

"He's been defying me and every teacher in the school for three or four years," he said.

"How do you know that?"

"It's in his cumulative record," the teacher replied.

"Okay, but what does Tim *actually* do?"

"Well," the teacher said, hesitating for a few moments, "he doesn't have any work to turn in at the end of the day."

"Shall we call that 'not having any work to turn in at the end of the day' instead of 'defiance'?" I suggested.

The teacher, somewhat surprised, agreed.

"When Tim hasn't any work to turn in at the end of the day," I said, "what do *you* do?"

"I fall apart. Actually, I shout at him and sometimes I pound on the desk," the teacher replied.

"What might happen if you did *not* fall apart?"

"Well, I can't let him get away with that, can I?" the teacher protested. "What kind of teacher would I be?"

"It appears to me that Tim has been getting away with things for three or four years now. Every afternoon at about the same hour, Tim seems to destroy an adult. Do you agree?"

He did agree. And he also agreed to try *not* falling apart.

Some weeks later, the teacher—surprised and delighted—telephoned me to say that not only had he changed his thinking and overt behavior, but that Tim was beginning to turn in his schoolwork!

The teacher's report really didn't surprise me because Tim, receiving no rewards for not turning in his work, now had a better chance to change.

I believe the change in Tim's behavior was predictable.

Once the teacher began to think operationally, dealing not with the abstraction "defiance," but with the reality of Tim's "not turning in schoolwork every afternoon," he was able to see that the more immediate question for him was not *Tim's* behavior but *his own.* When he changed his way of behaving, Tim was provided with the conditions to change his.

I recall another teacher who complained in a school workshop I was conducting that she was troubled by what she called a "hyperactive student."

She said she needed help. She did not know how to handle the child's "hyperactivity."

"Is this a medical diagnosis?" I asked.

"No," she replied, "But he has been checked by his family doctor."

"What does the child do?" I asked her.

"He's afraid," she said, "and he's so anxious all the time."

"But what does he *do*?"

"Well, he's acting out," she said.

"These are interpretations! What does the child actually do? Describe his behavior for me. What do you observe him doing?"

"He wiggles around in his seat," she said, "and he fidgets all over the place."

"What happens when he wiggles in his chair, when he fidgets?"

"I get upset," she replied.

Again, I suggested that the teacher concentrate on *her own* concepts and behavior rather than on what she called, in the abstract, the child's "hyperactivity." She did, and weeks later she could say that she was responding in more appropriate ways to the child's behavior in class.

Taking responsibility for her own behavior was possible when she started looking at her relationship with the child in literal terms. Indeed, once she concentrated on *her* behavior, she reported a change in the child's responses in her presence.

Both of these vignettes illustrate much more than just operational definitions, and I want to explore the process of self-responsibility more fully in a later chapter.

For now, let's look at some of those other words that probably are on most lists of attributes of good relationships.

"Trust" is such a word.

A father stopped me one day on campus to talk about his son, a former student of mine at the university.

"I'm having a real problem with Jim," the father said, "I can't trust him anymore."

We talked for some time about "trust" as an abstraction.

"What do you do when you trust somebody?" I asked him.

After several minutes and some discussion, he was able to define "trust" operationally: "I 'trust' people when I think I can predict what they are going to do." Other people's operational definitions might include thinking that whatever the other does will be in my best interest or believing the other will do what I want.

Under what conditions would the father *not* "trust"? He answered very quickly by saying, "I suppose it's when those people don't do what I want them to do or when I'm not sure of what they're going to do." This seemed to surprise him.

I suggested that the father and I role-play his situation in two ways—I would play the part of son Jim.

We used "trust," the abstraction, in the first situation.

"Jim, I can't trust you anymore," the father said.

"What do you want me to do, Dad?" I answered.

The father listed two or three things that he expected from Jim.

"But I don't want to do that," I replied.

The father smiled. "Yes," he said, "that's what's been happening at home."

I suggested the alternate procedure, using *his operational definition* of "trust."

"I can't predict your behavior anymore, Jim," the father said.

"You mean there's something that you want to happen, is that right, Dad?" I replied. "And what you want to happen may not be what I want to happen," I continued. "And if I don't do what you want, I am somehow not 'trustworthy' by your definition."

The father saw that the problem actually was his, not

Jim's. He could be responsible only for his own behavior, just as Jim could be responsible only for his. A different teaching tool was needed.

Another of the most used abstractions is the hypothetical construct "love."

I grew up, as most people do, making a beautiful and all-important word out of "love" without defining it operationally.

Five members of a family attended my seminar to talk about what was happening in their home. The mother claimed there was too much friction; family members were not getting along with one another.

I suggested that each of the family members express one thing they could do in the coming week to change the situation.

Mother spoke first.

"I think we could be happier if we each 'loved' one another more," she said.

The other members of the family agreed.

"What would you literally do?" I asked.

"We'd each put the other person first," the father suggested.

Again, everyone in the family agreed. They suggested that they had developed an operational definition of "love."

My response was that their idea sounded great, of course, but that I didn't think it could work. I thought it was an impossible relationship to develop, and I said so.

I said that I thought I could demonstrate very simply that their solution was unworkable. Using the principle of putting the other person first, I asked them to *line up*.

They milled around for a few moments, and discovered that there really was no way to line up by "putting the other person first."

They were ready to agree that two people could not love one another simultaneously in the way they had suggested. They realized the meaninglessness of their definition and began to talk with one another more in terms of specific operational events.

Since then, I have used this illustration in several seminars and classes. Sometimes I make a deal with a volunteer that we will each "love" one another by "putting the other person first."

We try to demonstrate. I ask the volunteer to stand, and I stand behind him only to find that he continues to stand in front of me. Then, when I point out that he had previously agreed to put *me* first, his response usually is something to the effect that he enjoys being first!

In class on one occasion, my students said they knew of a way to avoid this dilemma. "Let's form a circle," they suggested, "and that way no one will be first and no one will be last."

"You have a point," I replied, "but I wonder what would happen if you tried to go through the cafeteria line like that?"

Another of those list-words is, predictably, "confidence."

College students often come to me to express what they call their "lack of confidence."

I usually begin by asking what would have to happen for them to see themselves as having "confidence."

One young man said that if he had more "confidence," he would ask a girl for a date.

"So, your problem is not you lacking confidence, it's you lacking a date!" He agreed.

"Fine," I replied. "Let's not work on 'confidence' then, let's work on you asking a girl for a date."

He agreed.

"What might happen if you ask a girl for a date?"

"Well, she might not go," he said.

"What else might happen?"

"I guess she might say yes," he replied.

"Suppose she does turn you down. What will you think?"

"I guess I'd feel really put down," he said. "You've learned to think depreciating thoughts about yourself in such a situation. You *could* think something else, couldn't you?"

"Like what?"

"You could think 'Well, I'd like her to have gone out with me. I regret she's going to miss out on the opportunity.'"

I then suggested that he make a list of three or four girls who he would be willing to date. I asked him to include those girls who were not married or going steady or in some other way "spoken for."

Then I suggested that he agree to telephone one girl and that if she refused he immediately would call another on his list.

I have used this procedure several times, asking the student to make the telephone calls from my office during his interview time. So far, I haven't had one young man in this circumstance leave my office without a date.

Once a student who says he lacks "confidence" defines the situation in operational terms, he is able to describe several ways of behaving in regard to the situation that is troubling him. And he is able to do something about the problem.

Words are indeed fantastic tools; without them, we'd probably still be in caves. But words are not realities, even though they are often confused with realities.

I know that my relationships with other people have improved enormously since I began to speak operationally. I remember when I did not articulate operational definitions. I hoped that other people would somehow figure out what I wanted to happen. The truth was that they frequently did not. And much of the time I'm sure that even I didn't know clearly what I wanted to happen.

Same Word, Different Meaning?

Operational definitions are not in the dictionary. They are individual. For example, one person might define "romance" operationally as a candlelight dinner in an expensive, chic restaurant. To another person, the operational definition of "romance" might be what literally happens after dinner at home when the lamps are turned low in the den. If the two speak only of "romance," their messages to one another may be unclear. If they speak of events and happenings, what they want to take place at least will be understood.

When I communicate operationally, what I want to happen is clearer to all those involved. When I communicate operationally, I also am clarifying the possibility of whether or not what I want to happen *can* happen.

I consulted recently with a corporate executive who wanted to know why his interdepartmental communications were not being understood.

I asked him to show me some recent memos he had sent out. One after another showed word-abstractions rather than operational definitions. A memo to the shipping department read: "I expect more loyalty from your department."

"What," I asked the executive, "do you want the people in the shipping department to do? What do you want to happen there?"

"For one thing," he said, "I want to be sure that when I call the shipping department at seven thirty in the morning, someone will answer the telephone."

"Suppose you simply said *that*," I suggested. "Then both you and the people in the shipping department will be clearer on what you want to happen."

Not long ago I was reading a magazine published by a national organization for industrial editors. An editorial commented that "more trust" should be communicated to employees through company newspapers and magazines.

I can imagine the reaction of many who read this editorial. Their reaction probably was that they knew what "trust" was; the editorial made sense to them. But I wonder if it did. I wonder if they know, operationally, what "trust" is. I wonder if they could describe it in events and happenings so that the message is clear.

Other examples from all walks of life are legion.

What does a military general want to happen when he

asks for "loyalty" or "integrity"?

What does a politician want to happen when he suggests that you put more "trust" in him?

What does the minister want to happen when he calls for you to have more "faith"? What does he want you to do, literally?

Incidentally, I might add that nouns are most frequently nonoperational as opposed to verbs, which are more likely to be operational. You might try turning nouns into verbs to make greater sense from what is happening in a specific situation. For example, instead of saying "I am mad at you," try describing what is happening this way: "I am 'madding' at you." This may help you think in terms of what you are actually doing.

Return to the list you made at the beginning of this chapter. Consider your relationship with a specific person—your spouse, a son or daughter, your fiance, a friend or neighbor, employee or employer. Instead of using abstract words to define the attributes of the relationship, try thinking in terms of behavior, actual events and happenings. And the next time you want John or Mary to have "consideration" for you, choose not to use that abstract term. Instead, tell John or Mary what you want to happen. What is it that you want one or the other to literally do?

Now, I'd like you to look with me at two other words-- "happy" and "unhappy."

What is literally happening when you describe yourself as "happy"?

When I say I am "happy," usually I am saying that things are going the way I want them to go. To me that's one appropriate definition of the word "happy," and it may seem appropriate to you also.

"Unhappy," then, is when things are *not* going the way I want them to go.

When things aren't going the way I want them to go, I have learned to behave in certain ways to get them to go the way I want them to.

Have you learned that too? I suspect you have.

Before you read on, think about what you do and what others do in order to get their way.

three

Get-My-Way Behavior

If someone had asked me a few years ago to make a list of what I did or what other people do when things weren't going the way we wanted them to, I probably would have included crying or pouting, and perhaps screaming, shouting, pushing, plus announcing an occasional alleged headache or backache.

Some of these ways of behaving may be on *your* list now.

Your list also might include such statements and questions as these: "If you had a childhood like mine, you'd drink too" and "What do you expect from someone who has to work these kinds of hours?"

When I was young, I learned many ways of getting my way. Most of us do. In fact, the techniques probably are as varied and creative as there are people in the world.

Words can be used as get-my-way tools. Those words that I discussed in Chapter 2 frequently are get-my-way words in the sense that I want someone to do something after I have used them.

When Jim's father told Jim he could not "trust" him

anymore, he was attempting to change his son's behavior, to have happen what the father wanted to happen. The father used the abstraction "trust" wanting to get his way.

He and I (and you) undoubtedly learned to do this when we were children and our parents said things such as "If you really 'loved' me, you would clean up your room . . . . If you really 'cared,' you'd be home by nine o'clock . . . . If you were really 'considerate,' you'd help wash the dishes."

Notice that the "loving," the "caring," the "consideration" are get-my-way tools. They are also nonoperational abstractions that are seen as *motives* we tend to believe in as "things."

We were taught to "do" something when an abstraction was used in this way. The obligation to perform—which we call "motive"—was thrust upon us by someone else.

I was in a supermarket recently and witnessed a mother "teaching" (unknowingly, I'm sure) her young daughter how to get her way.

The child was in a stroller. Suddenly, she spied some candy on a shelf and pointed to it. She wanted some. But her mother told her that she couldn't have any because it was nearly lunchtime.

The child began to cry. She cried louder as her mother began pushing the stroller farther from the candy shelf, and finally the child threw a rattle to the floor and began stomping her feet on the bottom of the stroller.

Within a few seconds, the mother abruptly stopped the stroller, turned it around, returned to the candy shelf and gave her daughter some of the candy that she wanted. The daughter stopped crying almost immediately.

Many of my colleagues—looking for a motive—might say that perhaps the child had a familial deprivation of love. I would have to say that the child simply wanted candy. Some of my colleagues also might say that the mother, in submitting, demonstrated a weak ego structure. I believe she simply wanted her daughter to be quiet.

The two worked up a deal, and they both achieved what they wanted at that moment.

The child received her candy. The mother received quiet.

At thirty or even sixty, the grown-up "child" still may be making similar deals with her family and others, getting paid off just as effectively.

Most get-my-way techniques can be lumped under three broad headings: helplessness, suffering, and anger. These are learned responses to interpersonal situations that aren't going the way we want them to go.

Robert McKinley, a psychiatrist in San Antonio, used these broad headings in his book *The Complete Neuroticist* (New York, Pageant Press International Corp.), published in 1969. As I explore them with you in this chapter, I'll try to look at them in an operational sense.

Helplessness

Obviously, there are times when we are really "helpless." We may be helpless in the face of death, which we cannot fully understand. And we are helpless physically at times, as when an object twice our weight is resting on top of us.

But more often than not, in interpersonal relationships, helplessness is a learned way of inviting and sometimes manipulating other people to do what we want them to do, or not do what we don't want them to do.

Actual helplessness is seldom a reality in interpersonal relationships.

From an early age, we are taught to make excuses. We are taught that we are helpless, and we spend much of our lifetime going about giving people explanations for our helplessness.

Being sick can be a form of helplessness. As a college professor, I have had many students tell me that they had to miss an examination because of illness. Rarely have I had a student tell me he missed an exam because he was not prepared.

We sometimes talk ourselves into illness, perhaps to get our way.

In the last 100 years, ever since Sigmund Freud, we have fostered a form of helplessness in our culture. We have developed hypothetical constructs of helplessness, forces that seem to be beyond our control. And those hypothetical constructs offer us an excuse not to do something or a reason why our behavior ought to be accepted by others without question.

We learn to explain our behavior but not to change it.

I've heard people say things such as this: "How do you expect me to do better on my income?" or "I'm just that way, and I can't help it" or "I act that way because my mother did such and so when I was too little to know what was happening." "I am a victim."

Reasons and excuses appear to be in control of the individual.

The more traditional psychology, psychiatry and religion have done much to make us helpless, forever explaining "why" in past-tense terms and giving us reasons not to change our inappropriate behavior.

Most of us have known someone very "religious" who might typically say something such as "I can't do anything unless God does it through me." In other words, if God had wanted this person to do something, God would have made him accomplish the task. This can be helplessness, a comfortable cop-out for not having done something.

And in psychology and psychiatry, witness the person who is caught up in "unconscious processes" beyond his control, "complexes" from his childhood which become powerfully compelling excuses for change (or no change) in behavior. And in the '90s, it's the genes!

Incidentally, it might be noted, the more "helpless" the client or patient, the more important the "helper"!

When I claim helplessness, I am trapping myself inside a box. I give up self-responsibility; I sell out to an internal process, a kind of a demon, larger than I am.

Past-tense explanations are not the same as present-tense explanations, a difference which I will develop more completely in Chapter 5.

Suffering

As with helplessness, there are many "suffering" behaviors. One of the most common forms sounds something like this: "You've hurt my feelings." In other words, I am hurting, and you did it. You are responsible; I am not.

When I tell you that you have hurt my feelings, what is

it that I want to happen? I want an apology, probably. But I want something more than just words that say "sorry." I also want a change in your behavior. I want you to act differently, more to my expectations. Once you change whatever you are doing that I don't like, then I don't have to hurt anymore. As a matter of fact, if you comply, you have just agreed to let me control you with my "feelings."

Following along in this example, I find it especially interesting that at first I am admitting that the other person has controlled me ("you" have hurt my feelings). But then I change the whole situation around to get control of the other person by his accepting responsibility for my "feelings."

This is manipulation in interpersonal relationships, something that we learn to do in childhood and continue doing as long as it seems to work.

Another form of suffering is behaving "shy." Shyness is a learned response in interpersonal relationships. No one is born shy.

When I display my shyness (by doing those well-known behaviors called "shy"), I am really trying to get someone else to do something. I want them to recognize my existence or treat me in a certain way, a way which I consider best. If they meet my expectations, I can be happy. And if they don't, I can elect other reactions, including the predictable withdrawing, another way of expressing suffering.

When I withdraw, I wait for someone to find me and to revise whatever behavior they were exhibiting when I ran away. If they change, I have had my way. They have done what I wanted them to; I have won control.

Sometimes this kind of withdrawing isn't enough, and the next step may be attempted suicide or perhaps suicide itself; permanent withdrawal.

A number of people every year contemplate suicide not because of terminal illness, for example, but simply because things aren't going the way they want them to go interpersonally. When I talk with someone who is considering such a drastic step, I usually begin by asking a few questions.

For example: "How do you intend to kill yourself?" "Who do you want to find you?" "What isn't that person doing that you want him to do?" "What is happening that you don't like?"

Once he is able to answer these questions, he usually can see that he is simply trying to get something to happen. He can understand that he is blocked in what he considers very significant areas of life, and that he wants a change. With this insight, he may be ready to look for alternative ways of responding to these situations, ways he can accomplish himself without depending upon the changed behavior of other people.

If, however, the suicide actually does occur, those who remain are left to deal with the event, thus continuing the transaction even after the final withdrawal.

Of interest regarding suicide are the findings I heard reported some years ago by a coroner of a large city. He concluded that a rather significant percentage of actual suicides he had investigated were apparently not really intended, but that the deed was completed when procedures went awry accidentally.

In our culture, one of the most common forms of suffering is to worry. Worry is a kind of "voodoo" system, a suffering in advance. We learn at an early age that if we worry, we might be able to cause something to happen or to prevent something from happening.

Consider the high school student whose mother worries because he isn't home by ten o'clock at night. When he finally does arrive home, his mother predictably will tell him how she has been "worried to death" about his well-being and his whereabouts.

His mother's message is designed most likely to stimulate such thoughts as these during his next late night: Mother is home suffering, and I'm in a way responsible to do that which she expects me to do, to get home on time, and thereby reduce her suffering.

Many parents were taught that they have a responsibility to worry, that all *good* parents worry. They may even believe that they are required to stay awake until their son or daughter returns home.

Should they go to sleep before their child returns, thereby cutting off the worry, they assign responsibility to themselves for the accident or other problem which might occur. This is a kind of voodoo.

I have even heard parents say, after an accident twenty-five miles removed, "Had I only been awake, this might never have happened!"

McKinley has suggested that we could substitute the word "suffering" for the word "worry" whenever we use the latter. That way we can be a little clearer on what is really happening.

Jealousy also is worry, a form of suffering. In jealousy,

a person says, "I'm afraid something bad will happen." By worrying that the negative situation actually might occur, the individual creates an elaborate "voodoo" control system that he hopes might prevent what he doesn't want to happen.

The child in the supermarket was exhibiting a suffering behavior when she cried. She learned that she could get her way by crying, and that sometimes crying had to be extended into a tantrum to get what she wanted. Many people cry their way through life, tearfully "forcing" others to do what they want them to do... of course, only with the other's permission.

Crying, or any of the other get-my-way behaviors I've been discussing, are retained and used because they work in relation to certain others. They are ways of behaving that people use day in and day out, and are not usually malicious. Like language, they help us to get things we want.

More sophisticated than crying, but suffering nevertheless, is situational depression. While there are some known physiological and biochemical correlates to certain pervasive depression states, I believe that depression behaviors in interpersonal situations are often get-my-way tools. Again, not malicious, but learned and reinforced in earlier experiences.

I recall a man who came to me because he was situationally "depressed" at home.

The conversation went something like this: "When you are depressed," I said, "what is it that you do? How do you behave?"

"I sigh a lot, I put my head in my hands, and I think 'Isn't it awful,'" he replied.

"Who comes up to you and says 'What's the matter?'" I asked.

"My wife does, but—how did you know that happens?"

"Because I think you'll agree with me that it's not too productive to sit around with your head in your hands, sighing a lot, and thinking 'Isn't it awful' unless someone comes up to you and says 'What's the matter?'...and perhaps adds even more overt ministrations."

The man agreed.

By his depression behavior, the man was inviting some-one else to do what he wanted. He was suffering, to get something.

"By the way, do you do those same 'depressing' behaviors at work?", I asked. He responded with an emphatic "Never!"

Anger

This is the "last resort" technique, the heavy artillery reserved for the final try to get other people to do certain things. I have seen many examples of anger, both in myself and in other people. Anger behavior includes shouting, screaming, yelling, gesturing, swearing, slamming doors, driving erratically, and throwing things (sometimes lethal).

Anger may take the form of silence or of overt behavior which can often lead to physical attack.

The point to this discussion is that we all learn get-my-way techniques, behaviors that we hope will elicit from other people what we want them to do. Get-my-way behaviors are continued as long as they are rewarded, as long as they work and we get what we are after. The problem is that they are inappropriate because they require submission by another person. One person loses so that the other person can win, a concept to be dealt with in detail in Chapter 6.

The person who "sits around situationally depressed" will probably continue that behavior if people pay off for his actions or until he sees an alternative way of being happy.

That's what we all want, to be happy, to have things go the way we want them to go. Using helplessness, suffering, and anger, in my opinion, is not appropriate because it involves demands and manipulation, and often ends in frustration and broken relationships.

Responsibility for Feelings vs. Responding to the Shared Situation

Let's look at some other examples of get-my-way techniques.

Suppose the youngster in the stroller in the supermarket is now an adult. She might be a partner in a drama similar to one I heard about recently in a counseling situation.

The husband came to me to discuss his marriage. He said that he and his wife often disagreed heatedly.

I asked him to describe how he and his wife behaved when they disagreed.

"Usually, she runs into the bathroom and locks the door... and then she cries," he said.

"And what do you do?" I asked him.

"I usually stand on the other side of the door and try to talk her out. Most of the time it works, but I notice that I lose the argument by the time she's out," he said.

I explained to him that I believed his wife's behavior, while not malicious, was nonetheless her way of getting him to do what she wanted him to do. It seemed to me simply a behavior slightly more sophisticated than the child-in-the-stroller's behavior, a behavior that will continue as long as a payoff is forthcoming.

"What do you think you wife might do in the bathroom if you don't talk her out?" I asked him.

"She might do something dumb. She might hurt herself. She might even try to kill herself," he said.

I suggested to him that if his wife were really bent on taking her own life, she could do so when he was not present anytime. And I also suggested that he might consider changing his own behavior in some fashion that would allow his wife to consider changing hers.

After some discussion, he agreed to try.

A few weeks later, the husband returned to tell me what had happened.

Another heated disagreement had erupted and, predictably, the wife ran into the bathroom, locked the door, and cried.

Here's what the husband did this time. He went to the bathroom door and said, "Betty, I'm aware we aren't able to talk right now. I'm going down to the drugstore to get a cup of coffee. I'll be back in about thirty or forty minutes. I hope we'll be able to talk then."

With that, the husband departed the house, to return in a half hour or so.

"When I came back, she was out of the bathroom and

calmed down. We could talk, and we worked things out," he said.

What happened was this: when the husband changed his behavior so that he was no longer paying off his wife's get-my-way techniques, he was inviting his wife to modify her way of dealing with the situation.

She was relieved of completing the old scenario and provided an opportunity to do differently.

She was disarmed. She was not defeated.

There was no reason for the wife to sit alone in the bathroom, crying to an empty house. The husband refused to be controlled by his wife's sobbing, and they were able to encounter one another reasonably and with less emotion (fewer get-my-way behaviors).

On another occasion, a woman told me that she came home from work one evening to find her husband silently pouting and unwilling to respond to her greetings. She said, "Are you alright?" The silent pouting continued, but with a slight shrug, and a "pained" expression.

What do you suppose she said?

If she had said, "What's the matter? Is something wrong? " She would have fallen neatly into the husband's learned get-my-way system.

Instead, she chose another alternative. She thought to herself: My husband appears to be communicating that things aren't going the way he wants them to, and I'm somehow involved.

So, she said, "Bill, what do you want to happen?"

Once he told her, she could then decide whether or not she wanted to participate in whatever her husband wanted.

And she could also say, "Look, next time, just tell me what you'd like to have happen. I'd really prefer that to all that silent pouting and 'guess what I'm thinking' business."

That's real change in a relationship, and it perhaps demonstrates how this particular relationship might survive while others, based on get-my-way techniques, might not.

Do you recall Tim, the "defiant" student, in Chapter 2? Tim didn't have any schoolwork to turn in at the end of the day and in response to that his teacher would shout and pound on the desk, both "angry" responses to the interpersonal situation. Once the teacher stopped reinforcing his behavior, Tim was able to change what he was doing. He was able to modify his own behavior. He began turning in his schoolwork at the end of the day just as his classmates were doing.

When I use a get-my-way tool, I am really setting up a situation by which I ask someone else to be responsible for my feelings.

Conversely, when I respond to someone else's get-my-way tools, I am permitting myself to become responsible for the way other people tell me they feel.

A child learns this at an early age when a parent says "You'd make me happy if you'd do such and such" or "Do this and that or you'll make Daddy angry" or "Play nice or your friends won't come back."

The youngster suddenly is responsible for the parent's happiness or lack of it. He is responsible for Daddy's anger. He is responsible for making his friends happy so they will want to remain friends.

He is taught to feel guilty if he doesn't keep others happy.

In other words, if he doesn't accept the responsibility for doing what he's supposed to do, then the next requirement is to feel guilty and to tell someone else that he feels that way.

Feeling Guilty vs. Being Guilty

To the child, or even to an adult, feeling guilty out loud can be a secondary tool in itself, to get someone off his back, perhaps even himself if he is internalizing the situation.

In college counseling, I often talk with parents who have discovered that their son or daughter is experimenting with marijuana or is taking some other drug. Sooner or later, one of the parents will claim that "John doesn't even feel guilty." And I will say: "Do you want John to stop smoking marijuana, or do you want him to feel guilty?" Frequently, the parents aren't sure.

Because the parents themselves were taught to be responsible for other people's feelings, they undoubtedly taught John to do the same. John is supposed to feel guilty now; his parents expect that he will. And if he doesn't, the parents are aware of something not happening that they believe should happen.

Because things aren't going the way they want them to go, they quite likely will choose to "fall apart," to become helpless, to suffer, or to become angry.

If so, they are trying to elicit from the offspring responsibility for feelings rather than responsiveness to the situation.

I often have heard parents encouraged to express their feelings to a child: "Tell your child you're bothered by what he's doing." Notice that in doing so, the parent is teaching the child that the primary issue is the parent's "bother," not the child's behavior. It then follows that when the parent is not present to be "bothered," the behavior may not need to be evaluated.

The more appropriate alternative, once again, is focusing on the behavior rather than on the feeling.

Suppose I'm walking down the street one evening, and I discover an injured man lying in the gutter. I can suffer out loud about the victim's sad state of affairs and feel guilty that society has forced this man into a desperate and inhuman situation.

Or I can take the man to the hospital, see that he is cared for, and then go on my way.

In the first alternative, I am attempting to be responsible for feelings. In the second alternative, I am being responsive to the situation.

The Bible tells of the Good Samaritan who chose to be responsive to the situation. He also found an injured man one day. He bound the man's wounds, took him to an inn, paid for his lodging, and then departed.

In class, I have illustrated the difference between trying to be responsible for feelings and being responsive to the situation this way: "If any of you come on campus some day and find that a tree has fallen down on me, don't shout 'Oh, that must hurt!' I would much prefer that you tried to move the tree. Be responsive to the situation."

Students often visit with me near the end of the university's semester to talk about their grades. Many of those interviews begin with students saying that they feel guilty about their poor marks.

"To whom do you feel guilty?" I ask.

"To myself, I suppose, and also to Mother and Dad," is the typical reply.

"You believe you've let them down?"

"Yes, that's about it," one student says.

"Have you already mailed the letter home?"

"How do you know I've mailed a letter home?"

"Because it's predictable. I'll bet I know what you said, too. You said something such as 'I know I've let you down. You've sacrificed and done without just to keep me in school, and now I've disappointed you. There must be something wrong with me. I'm going to the psychologist to find out what.'"

In the discussion which follows, I attempt to show the student how he has employed his get-my-way techniques and has set up Mother and Dad with his expressed feelings of guilt. They will predictably, feel required to respond to their son's misfortune and will say so in a telephone call of forgiveness within a day or so. That will get their son off the hook; he no longer must feel guilty for bad grades. Because he's been "forgiven," he sees no reasons to change his behavior, and his grades likely will not improve.

Neither the student nor his parents have been responsive to the situation. Instead, they have traded responsibility for their feelings.

Feeling guilty is designed to encourage someone to forgive you, which, incidentally, really gives you permission to do whatever you did again.

It works this way: I say, "Oh I'm so sorry." Traditionally

you reply, "Oh that's OK." Well, if it's OK, I can do it again!

Being guilty, on the other hand, is different. When I am guilty, I am recognizing behavior that I might want to change.

The student with poor grades was guilty of inappropriate behavior--not going to class, not studying enough, not taking adequate notes, not preparing for the examinations. He could change those ways of behaving if he wished to do so. The chances of his doing so are practically nil so long as he avoids self-responsibility by allowing his parents to be responsible for his feelings and he responsible for theirs.

I appreciate the Biblical story concerning the woman about to be stoned to death for her sins. Jesus said that the person in the crowd who was without sin should throw the first stone, and no one did. Then Jesus told the woman to go on her way and not repeat her inappropriate behavior. He didn't suggest that she feel guilty, or that she fret about what she had done, but rather that she simply stop the behavior.

Perhaps it's good theology to say that the way to get one's sin forgiven is to confess, repent, and stop the sinning, in contrast to what seems to be more popular—confess, repent, and repeat it! Which illustrates the point that in our culture, at least, if we feel guilty out loud sufficiently, we tend to be forgiven. At any rate that's our training.

Those old enough to remember the Watergate affair recall many who wanted so badly for Richard Nixon to "feel guilty" out loud. They also recall Judge Sirica implying that Gordon Liddy received the longest sentence because he showed no remorse!

Not long ago, I was discussing these ideas with a ladies church group, and I introduced them to what I call the "covered dish syndrome." This is reflected in the behavior of some of the women of the church who take hot dishes to people in need, perhaps when there has been a death in the family. Like the Good Samaritan, these ladies may be responding to the situation. But some may not be.

If one lady takes her offering in an expensive china bowl that requires taping her name to the bottom, rather than a throw-away container, she may be ensuring that the recipient will know who brought the food.

As a matter of fact, when this lady arrives at her neighbor's home and observes several other dishes on the table brought by other friends, to leave hers might not be being responsive to the situation. But after all, she does want her friend to know she "cares" and has made an effort.

Simply put, I have learned (as you probably did) to expect other people to attempt to control me. I have also learned (as you did) to attempt to control those other people. Neither is really appropriate.

One year I received a robot for Christmas. He had a box of buttons that made him move forward, backward, right and left. Each human being has a "box of buttons" that he learns to give away. He also learns to accept the buttons of another person. We give away responsibility for ourselves, and we become responsible for other people. We expect that they will act in certain ways and say certain things. And when they don't, when they do not meet our expectations, we often "fall apart," manifesting our get-our-way behaviors—some form of helplessness, suffering, or anger.

Wouldn't it be delightful if we each pushed just our own "buttons?"

During the years since the first edition of this book, a new movement has popularized the terms co-dependency and enabling. For me, enabling simply refers to one's rewarding inappropriate behaviors in another, probably to avoid some helplessness, suffering or anger by the other. Co-dependency, in the context of this book, is operationally defined as two people actively accepting responsibility for each other's feelings rather than responding rationally to their shared situations. Think about that.

Each person in a relationship has several choices of how he can behave, depending on the options he has learned. Basically, he can behave either appropriately to the shared situation or otherwise. If his partner chooses to behave inappropriately, he need not respond in like manner. He has the prerogative to select behavior that is more effective and worthwhile for him and thus for both.

Suppose one afternoon two strangers are walking along the street toward one another.

One of them bumps into the other, accidentally.

"Excuse me," Mr. A says.

"Of course," Mr. B replies.

The two men go their separate ways, and the incident is forgotten.

What might happen if Mr. A says nothing?

Mr. B may become visibly upset. He may stop to stare at the departing Mr. A. He may even curse or flash a gesture of disapproval, an ungentlemanly last word to a relatively minor incident now blown out of all appropriate proportion.

Mr. B's expectations have not been met. A stranger, Mr. A, has not done what he is "supposed" to do. Suddenly, Mr. A has become responsible for Mr. B's feelings. (Make up your own examples here from the world of driving our roads and freeways!)

The simple word "feelings" offers all sorts of problems in our relationships with other people. I believe the problem is that we fail to update the word as we grow into adulthood. The word "feelings" becomes a misnomer.

We develop "myths" about feelings, and that's what I want to discuss in Chapter 4.

four

The Myths of Feelings

Do Feelings Cause Behavior?

When I'm driving down the street and I notice another car in my lane coming toward me, I may experience many things happening in my body. My pulse may quicken, my hands perspire, and my muscles tighten. These are physiological responses to a perceived situation typically described not in these physical terms but as the experience of *feeling* scared or frightened.

Operationally, I would be clearer and more accurate if I described what is really happening: "I am perspiring, my heart is beating faster, and my muscles are tense."

I've learned to think "scared" or "frightened" with the presence of these correlated physical occurrences. Each of us experiences visceral reactions which occur in response to the stimulus of a particular situation, like seeing the car on a path coming toward us. We have also learned to tie these occurrences to an abstract symbol. The problem is that we tend to make the abstract symbol the reality, and we call that a feeling. In actuality, we don't *feel* scared or frightened, we *think* and physically react scared or frightened.

In addition to making the abstract symbol the reality, we often behave in certain ways *because* of that so-called reality. For example, the common assumption is that when a person is angry he does something *because* of the anger. He might slam the door, and he might claim that "anger" made him do it. To me, slamming the door *is* the anger. It is angering behavior.

This is not a new view. Many readers may be familiar with the James-Lange theory of the emotions and the often quoted line that demonstrates that theory: "We are not running because we are afraid; we are afraid because we are running." An essay by William James written in 1884 ("What Is Emotion?") further describes this theory of emotions. "Common sense," James writes, "says we lose our fortune, are sorry and weep; we meet a bear, are frightened and run; we are insulted by a rival, are angry and strike." The James- Lange hypothesis states that this sequence is not correct. James writes that "the one mental state is not immediately induced by the other, the bodily manifestations must first be interposed between, and the more rational statement is that we feel sorry because we cry, angry because we strike..." He also writes: "Our natural way of thinking about these standard emotions is that the mental perception of some fact excites the mental affection called the emotion, and that this latter state of mind gives rise to the bodily expression."

Sometimes, as we all know, in emergency situations the process is so rapid and the protective response is so quick that we do not experience "fright" until after the crisis, when the physiological changes have finally had time to occur.

There *are* actual physiological feelings, of course.

When I was a youngster, I explored my world through physiological events called feelings, namely pressure, pain, cold, and warm. These are areas of scientific study in physiology and psychology. As I grew older, I continued to use the word "feelings," but I carried it over to what, probably could better be described intellectually in terms of thinking. Most people fall into this same trap.

I'm sure you have heard people say things such as "What do you *feel* the Astro's chances are to win the pennant?" or "Do you *feel* this product will sell?" or "Do you *feel* you know what's going to be on the examination?" In each case, the more appropriate word is not "feel" but "think." The process is intellectual.

This misuse of the abstract symbol often makes interpersonal relationships more difficult, and I believe I can demonstrate this in discussing what I call the four myths of feelings. Most people practice these myths; perhaps you do too.

Are Feelings Involuntary?

The first myth is that feelings are involuntary, that they happen to us without forewarning, no matter what we do.

I'm sure you've heard someone say "I'm angry, and I just can't help it." The person really is saying that he has a right to be angry under these particular circumstances, and that anyone in the same situation also would be angry.

I don't think of feelings as being involuntary.

For example, a married couple is arguing. The argument becomes more heated. Both the husband and wife are shouting when suddenly the telephone rings. The man walks to the phone, picks up the receiver, and says, in a very pleasant voice, "Hello. Yes, this is George; so nice of you to call. Oh, she's just fine...We'd be delighted to come, and thank you for the invitation. It was nice of you to call. Good-bye."

He replaces the receiver, then returns to resume the argument in its original intensity. I wager you've done that yourself just as I have.

If the situation calls for it, we can replace overt angering with a more pleasant response. We can decide how to behave. After all, we don't know yet who's on the other end of the phone!

I think we learn that feelings are involuntary when we are children. What does a parent say to a child when the child is not getting what he wants for some reason? He might say something such as "I'm sure you must be very angry, and I don't blame you. I'd be angry too." The child is taught that anger is natural under the circumstances. It is logical and to be expected.

Robert McKinley, the psychiatrist, tells a poignant story of a youngster, two or three years of age, who is experiencing a severe thunderstorm for the first time. The child is playing in his room and he hears a large clap of thunder. The parent in the next room calls out: "Are you OK?"

The child, quite naturally, thinks to himself that for some reason, probably because of the thunder, he's not supposed to be OK.

"Why?" He calls back from his room.

"Didn't you hear that thunder? Aren't you afraid?"

And, he thinks, I *guess* I am afraid. I'm *supposed* to be afraid of the thunder.

In the future when a storm produces more severe thunder and lightning, the child—now afraid—rushes to his parent and is comforted. The parent has taught the child to be afraid of thunder. Fear is part of the thunder, and he soon learns that fear and perhaps other feelings are involuntary.

Parents often assume that their children should have the same feelings that the parents have been taught to have, and rather than teach the child to handle the situations, they teach him to feel as they did or do.

A youngster may be taught to fear snakes through his father's fear of snakes. If he is thus taught, he is likely to have certain reactions when he sees a snake. He will "think" snake, and there will be a correlated, physiological printout that may include a quickening of his heartbeat, increased flow of perspiration and perhaps even nausea. He will say he "feels" frightened. He may think he has no other choice.

However, if he learns more about snakes, which ones are dangerous and which ones are harmless, his physiological responses may be modified by these new experiences. A diamondback rattler might call up the old printout of nausea, sweating, and increased pulse rate, but he may respond to the situation differently rather than "feel" fear. He may experience the same physiological printout—the "fear," as he calls it—but he can respond more effectively to the situation because of his additional learning. Eventually the feeling of fear (actually the behavior of fear) will be extinguished by the repetition of the stimulus without some associated negative happening which he now understands better.

And upon recognizing a garter snake, he probably won't experience much physiological change at all because he has learned that garter snakes are not dangerous.

The change is in the "feeling" reaction occasioned by new learning, that is, in the way the youngster *thinks.*

So, although most of us are taught that feelings are involuntary, I think it can readily be shown that they are not. I *decide* how to behave in any situation as I have learned to do. If I am to change how I behave, therefore, I have to learn some new options.

Are Feelings Caused by Something Outside?

The second myth is that feelings are caused by something outside ourselves.

A student once told me that he was having trouble getting to his 8 A.M. class.

"I just can't get up for my eight o'clock," he said.

"Does some actual force keep you in bed?" I asked him.

"Well, no."

"Then I'd like you to change one word in your original sentence. Try saying 'I *don't* get up for my eight o'clock class.'"

The word "can't," I explained, implies an outside force, a kind of demon or spirit or monster of some type that has the student in his grip.

"What might happen," I said to the student, "if you did go to your eight o'clock class?"

"Well, I might get called on for my Spanish assignment, and I wouldn't like that," he said.

No outside force prevented the student from getting to his

eight o'clock class, but I believe he was using a get-my-way behavior. The payoff was not having to face the professor or the class. The strategy was to blame the problem on an outside force that made the student helpless.

Perhaps you've heard someone say "*You* have made me angry."

In other words, an outside force--another person--has visited anger upon this individual.

This is another example of using feelings as a get-my-way behavior. The person really is saying "I am angry, and it's your fault. Change what you are doing so I won't have to be angry anymore."

Few interpersonal forces render us actually helpless. And, because we can choose how we behave from among the learned options, the more accurate response might be that "I am responding in the only way I have learned to react to what you have done" or "I have decided to behave to what you have done by this option from among those I possess."

Notice the pronoun "I," the first person singular. Using "I" stresses that the speaker is responsible for his own selection of choices from among those he has learned. This is a crucial point that I will discuss later in more detail.

Consider a father after a difficult day, settling in his den to watch the evening news. Just as he is getting comfortable his children, six and eight years of age, come into the room doing what youngsters their age do—teasing one another, playing a game and yelling.

The father jumps to his feet shouting at the youngsters. "You make me furious," he cries.

In attempting to get his children to be quiet so he can hear the news, he expresses "anger" which has "descended" upon him. He claims that the cause of that "anger" was something outside himself, his children's behavior.

The more accurate description might have sounded this way: "I have decided to shout and complain in response to what you kids are doing wanting you to stop it."

There were other alternatives to what the father actually did. The father could have accepted the fact that the children were doing predictable, and therefore understandable, behavior to which he needn't have responded with anger. He could have had the children play in another room. *He* could have gone to another room. He could have decided to postpone his viewing and play with the children instead.

Other alternatives to his shouting were possible, but the father—believing, as most people do, that feelings are involuntary and are caused by something outside himself—rejected additional alternatives or refused to look for them.

And his shouting may have been successful. The option he selected undoubtedly was one that had worked for him before, or he would not have used it in this instance. Get-my-way techniques often work, and we continue using them because they do. The problem is that they may make our relationships with other people ineffective, awkward, and unclear as they require us to be helpless, to suffer, or to become angry. The fewer alternatives a person sees to a situation, the more limited he is in his response.

This matter of options or alternatives is a crucial one. In our culture, we often say a person is "sick" or "mentally ill" when he simply doesn't act the way we act. Some would claim he needs therapy. Could it not be that the person doesn't see the options we do or that we don't see the options he does? We may not be aware of the other's alternatives, and one of us may need to learn them. Perhaps we should call this *education* rather than *therapy*, with all its additional implications.

One December, a woman told me that she "couldn't help but be hurt when her daughter told her she wasn't coming home for Christmas."

The hurt, she claimed, was caused by something outside herself.

"You hurt me when you say that" indicates that the mother had *decided* to be hurt in response to the daughter's decision. It is understandable that the mother would like the daughter at home, but expressing the "hurt" was the mother's attempt to get her way, inviting the daughter to change what she was doing, in other words to come home for the holiday not because the daughter wanted to, but because she had been taught to be responsible for her mother's feelings.

Had the daughter changed her mind and come home, which she did not do, she would have been practicing what undoubtedly had been her early training. She would have complied with her mother's desires in order to prevent hurt to her mother and avoid guilt feelings in herself.

It's my belief that no one can directly transfer "hurt" to another person psychologically. One can provide a behavioral stimulus, but the other person must elect to be hurt by that stimulus. It is *his* decision.

If his training is such that he has only the one option to be hurt in the particular situation, then he will behave that way. The point is that there are options other than to be hurt. Those options must be learned.

I asked the mother to consider what might have happened if she hadn't been hurt.

"Well, I suppose the world wouldn't have come to an end," she said. "I probably would have had a more enjoyable Christmas, and so would my daughter. And I would have accepted my daughter's invitation to visit her for New Year's, instead of brooding and feeling rejected and let down." The mother was aware of other options, but she hadn't stopped to consider them.

Our feelings are not caused or controlled by things or persons outside ourselves without our permission.

Our training in terms of feelings is that we must have them and we must express them, which leads us to the third myth.

Can Feelings be Shared?

The third myth is that feelings can be shared.

Again, the crucial issue is what we think feelings are. For me, "feelings" may be redefined as the experiencing of the physiological changes occasioned by the perception of events in the context of the individual meanings assigned to those events. Thus, I *think* anger and I *feel* the physical correlates.

If I can learn to *think* differently, I will likely *feel* differently.

I can share words that I use to describe the physical reactions that I experience. When I do that, I am sharing my unique perception of those physical reactions I have. I'm talking now about my subjective reality.

My subjective reality cannot be shared directly with someone else's subjective reality. I can provide stimuli for the other person in the form of words, gestures, and other overt physical reactions, but the other person must experience these in his own unique way and make meaning of them in his own subjectivity.

Philosophers and psychologists call this realm of subjectivity the "phenomenological field" of the individual, and phenomenological fields cannot directly interact.

I am not denying that feelings as experiences are realities. Without question, these experiences occur subjectively. Because they do not exist in objective reality, they can't be shared.

Most of us attempt to share them anyway with hypothetical construct expressions such as "anger," "fear," "love," "hate," "rejection." These we say are the feelings shared.

We also often associate the words "like" and "dislike" with feelings. I propose a different view of these words to disconnect them from feelings and to recognize them as a means of evaluation. To say "I *like* something," then, means that I have a response somewhere on the positive side of my evaluation continuum. A *dislike* is on the negative side of the scale and more often reported out loud. These we *can* share!

The popularity of sensitivity training came about because many people believed feelings could be shared and indeed needed to be shared. They practiced a kind of "abscess theory." The approach was that the abscess of "anger" or "alienation" or whatever had to be "lanced"—

expressed—in order for healing to occur.

Many sensitivity sessions actually were instructional periods which frequently taught participants more skillful get-my-way techniques!

In a particular sensitivity group, a young man sobs. A typical approach would be to allow him to continue sobbing. Finally the group leader might say, "John, it seems as though you have some very deep feelings." And John continues crying, the sobbing becoming louder and louder, reinforced by the attention being given it.

Compare that approach with one in which someone says simply; "John, something must not be happening in your life that you want to happen. What is it?"

Now John isn't under the control of outside forces; he can decide how to behave. While he can share his sobbing (an operational event) and also his thoughts in words in response to the question and to the situation (another operational event), he cannot share feelings as defined above.

Can Others be Responsible for My Feelings?

The fourth myth is that we can be responsible for one another's feelings.

The subjective life of the individual is that and no more. What he experiences within himself in any situation is his alone. How he labels that experience is the result of what he has learned. It is uniquely his.

If he thinks that feelings are not involuntary and are not caused by something outside himself, then it follows that his behavior is a matter of choice among his learned options.

P.W. Bridgman suggested in *The Way Things Are* (Cambridge, Harvard University Press, 1959) that in writing scientific, papers, authors should use first person singular. Bridgman reasoned that because the scientist was the observer, he would write "I have observed such and such" rather than "It was observed that such and such happened."

Bridgman's idea is deceptively simple and enormously significant. No two people observe an event in quite the same way, and only by using the pronoun "I" can responsibility be assigned to the responsible person.

Philosophers for centuries have argued that each of us lives in a world of his own. And, as Bridgman wrote: "Not only do I see that I cannot get away from myself, but I see that you cannot get away from yourself. The problem of how to deal with the insight that we never get away from ourselves is perhaps the most important problem before us."

In interpersonal relationships, I believe first person singular is most appropriate because it places responsibility clearly.

If I say to another person, "*I* do not like what you did," then no contradiction is possible. No one can correct me because my perception of events and what I have decided to think about them is mine alone. The other person may, however, suggest that I received only a portion of the information, or that I received it unclearly for one reason or another. In such a case, the meaning of the message may be tentative until it can be negotiated. It also is legitimate for me to perceive the message quite differently from the way the other person perceives it.

On the other hand, if I say "*You* have made me angry,"

then "you" may very well contradict me by responding with something such as "No, I didn't." In fact, I am eliciting a defensiveness and also inviting "you" to attempt a control of me by your helplessness, suffering, or anger.

Only I am responsible for *my* behavior. Only I can change what I do. However, when I change my behavior, I may give the other person in the relationship the opportunity to evaluate his behavior and perhaps modify it.

In the example of the schoolteacher and his "defiant" student, Tim, in Chapter 2, when the schoolteacher concentrated on his behavior and not on Tim's, he sought to change himself. That destroyed the payoff (his angering behavior) which he had previously furnished Tim. Tim, within a few days, re-evaluated his own behavior and began changing it.

Unfortunately, most of us have learned to place the emphasis on the other person, to work on the behavior of other people rather than to concentrate on our own.

Get-my-way behavior is based on expressed feelings, such as helplessness, suffering, and anger. Such behavior is designed to convince the other person in the relationship that he is responsible and that he must change his behavior, what he is doing, so that I don't have to feel this way anymore.

Parents and teachers could contribute toward solving the problem of self-responsibility by encouraging youngsters to make more use of first person singular. This would help young people to experience their own unique and individual worlds and begin accepting responsibility for their own distinctive here-and-now experiences.

In consulting with businesspersons and educators, I have

noted how few of them write letters or memos to clients and associates in the first person singular. Every time "I" is avoided, there is the distinct possibility that we are avoiding experiencing ourselves and refusing to take responsibility for what we do.

When seen in the light of the discussion on these pages, the four myths of feelings in example form might sound like this:

    a. feelings are involuntary:

       "I feel angry and I can't help it."

    b. feelings are caused by something outside myself:

       "You caused it, and it's all your fault."

    c. feelings can be shared:

       "I've told you about it."

    d. we can be responsible for one another's feelings:

       "Now it's your responsibility to make me feel okay again."

Let me pose a question to you.

What is your definition of a "close" relationship?

Is it possible that your definition requires that you must practice the four myths of feelings?

If so, you may want to take another look at your definition. You may want to learn some new options.

five

Push vs. Pull

Why or What?

Edward, thirteen, is ushered into the principal's office. The principal, seated at his desk, is studying a report on Edward's behavior in seventh grade.

"Why did you do it, Edward?" the principal asks.

"I guess because I was angry. That's why I did it" is the answer.

Edward responded as he did probably to make his behavior more acceptable to the principal. Most of us have learned that "reasonable" cause makes the effect—in this case, Edward's behavior—more readily excusable.

More importantly, let's consider what Edward really was saying to the principal. I think he was saying that because of "anger" he had committed the inappropriate behavior. Anger was the motivating force. Edward, when he did whatever it was that he did, was under the control of anger.

Edward was using cause and effect to explain a happening. I've done this, and I'm sure you have also. Most of us fall into this habit, a practice I would like to question in this book. Unfortunately, most of us have been trained—as has Edward—to be more concerned with cause and effect than simply with the behavior, with what we are actually experiencing, events and happenings. I might even suggest that we have been trained to be better physicists than psychologists; physicists are the ones who are rightly concerned with cause and effect.

In the last chapter, I proposed that feelings typically are said to be the cause of something which is taking place. They become the motivation. These hypothetical constructs, these abstract symbols such as fear, trust, love, and others, are thought by many to catapult people into behaving in a certain way.

Such thinkers, I suggest, are *stimulus*-oriented rather than *experience*-oriented. They are concerned with *why* something took place rather than with *what* is literally happening.

B.F. Skinner deals with this issue in *Beyond Freedom and Dignity* (New York, Alfred A. Knopf, Inc., 1971). He relates an interesting example from Herbert Butterfield regarding Aristotle.

Aristotle observed that falling bodies accelerated as they fell. Of significance here is Aristotle's explanation for the acceleration. His conclusion was that a falling body accelerated because it possessed "more jubilance" as it approached its natural home.

Modern physicists would find this explanation ludicrous.

I would imagine that if Aristotle were to reappear he would readily accept the inadequacy of his earlier explanation. And he would probably recognize in other disciplines that we still use the same type of explanation he gave when he assigned "more jubilance" as causation in his theory.

In psychology, for example, I think we are doing the same thing as Aristotle did with jubilance when we assign such hypothetical constructs as aggression, alienation, and anxiety as explanations.

We often use abstract symbols—nonoperational concepts—to identify the motivation, the *why*. For example: "This person's *aggression* is a product of *anxiety* in the context of his *alienation*."

In the third chapter of this book, I gave the example of the child in her stroller in the supermarket. You'll remember that the child wanted some candy, and in order to get the candy she cried and screamed and threw her rattle to the floor. Mother undoubtedly wanted quiet, and so she eventually responded and gave her daughter the candy. They made a deal.

In Chapter 3 I suggested that some observers of this incident would say that the child suffered from a deprivation of familial love and that the mother obviously had a weak ego structure and that's *why* the child had a tantrum and *why* the mother gave in.

It's my contention that the child screamed and cried to get something... candy. And the mother responded as she did to get something else....quiet. It is more important to understand the purpose of the behavior than the abstract motive.

Past-tense "why" the child was throwing a tantrum and past-tense "why" the mother responded as she did are less significant to me than what the youngster was doing and what she was attempting to get as a result. The same can be said of the mother, for she was also trying to obtain something that she wanted.

You also may recall the college student who wanted more confidence. In that counseling situation, I could have spent hours trying to determine why the student lacked confidence. In the tradition of typical counseling practices I could have had several meetings with the student during which we would have explored his "feelings" and their development in order to explain his present predicament.

But again, I think the past-tense *why* (motives, hypothetical constructs) was not as important as the present-tense *what* (current happenings and wishes). The student wanted a date, you'll remember. Once that was clarified, he could work on getting what he wanted. I don't think it was necessary that he understand all of the nuances of his background that might have led to his hesitancy to ask girls for dates. Instead, he needed to be aware of what he already had learned relevant to this situation, and then learn some new procedures which would result in what he wanted to happen.

In the last chapter, I attempted to establish as a myth the idea that we are forced into a behavior as an effect of a cause. Instead, we do certain things in order to elicit some event which will follow our behavior.

I'm not saying that the past is irrelevant. One's past *is* significant. It provides structure and framework and, most important, learning. The past, however, is gone. It is unchangeable. What *can* be changed is what a person is doing now. He can learn new options, more alternative ways of behaving.

Motive or Purpose

I like to talk about the Pull Concept as opposed to the Push Concept. Much of traditional psychology and psychiatry is based on the Push Concept. This concept proposes that we are "pushed" into certain behavior by complexes, traits, needs, drives, feelings, etc. These are antecedents beyond our control. Therefore, our behavior is the effect of some cause under which we are helpless. From this position, a "treatment" process would include determining the cause, which usually requires long-term exploration.

As an analogy, consider our culture's medical model. When a doctor treats a physical disease such as appendicitis, he wants to treat the disease, not merely the symptoms. Traditional psychology attempts to do the same thing. The traditional psychologist, trained in the Push Concept, perceives the symptoms, the behavior, as only reflective of something "down deep" inside the person. That something is, he thinks, the real disease, and he calls it alienation, anxiety, or something similar. As I've said before, these are hypothetical constructs, not realities.

The Pull Concept seems much more appropriate. Here, a behavior is viewed not simply as an effect of something else but rather as a stimulus in itself to elicit something to follow. The Pull Concept requires that we understand behavior in terms of what comes *after* rather than what comes *before*. The get-my-way behaviors discussed in Chapter 3 are good examples.

So, under the Pull Concept, what we must deal with is what we traditionally have called symptoms, in operationally definable behavior, both overt and covert.

The original Freudian theory, a Push Concept, proposes that there is an ongoing battle in a nonoperational unconscious. The battle rages between and among alleged subdivisions of the unconscious, such as the id and superego, each also equally nonoperational in definition. The unconscious is conceived as a dynamic force which literally decides in a mysterious fashion the activities of a person's life without his permission or knowledge.

Instead of the unconscious, I prefer to think in terms of the *not-now conscious.*

The not-now-conscious aspect of the nervous system can be demonstrated simply by my asking you to think of your mother's first name. It's safe to assume that you weren't thinking of that name at the moment of stimulus, but that you probably could readily bring the name from your not-now conscious to your conscious awareness.

I think of the human nervous system as being much like a computer. (I suspect the computer designers conceived the reverse.) I recognize, of course, that at this writing we do not have a complete understanding of the brain and its total physiological activities. But my conception in analogy is that within each person's nervous system are informational bits, retained in memory-bank facility and which can be drawn upon when required. Bits have been retained and now are memory.

When we behave, we behave as we have *learned* to behave, following a printout of sorts.

One of the premises of this book is that we possess a facility to choose from among the options we have learned. We may learn more options to use now and again later in other situations. The not-now-conscious bits, including data from antecedent events, are in the nervous system and are available to us, but they are not controlling factors in themselves as was suggested by Freudian concepts.

The Pull Concept which I support reflects the operant conditioning theory held by such behaviorists as B.F. Skinner and by some behavior therapists who use these principles rather mechanistically. The distinction between the extremes of what they propose and what I propose is that I am not ready to delete consciousness and the facility to choose among learned options.

Some behavior modification adherents are saying that there is no internal control but, instead, simply a response to a stimulus. They contend that behavior modification occurs within the context of contingency changes in the environment without consciousness as a factor.

I don't deny that this process can occur, but I think each of us also is capable of selecting alternatives *consciously*. We can learn additional options. We can choose how we will behave within the limits that I've described. (I must add that I am very much aware that my viewpoint places me on both sides of a professional fence, as it were, when I describe myself as a "behavioral humanist." Nevertheless, that is my first person singular perception for now.)

I recall an attorney who once represented a man who had murdered several people in the presence of witnesses. In the courtroom, his client was judged to be insane at the time of the murders and was confined to a mental hospital. Some months later, he was pronounced cured and released.

When I asked the attorney what he had proved in the

courtroom, the attorney said he had demonstrated that the client "had not been himself."

And I asked him: "If your client wasn't himself, then who was he?"

I'm certain from the attorney's reaction to my question that he did not like its implications suggesting that the man had been possessed of a devil, helpless and somehow forced into a behavior over which he had no control. We both agreed that witchcraft was something better left to medieval times, but for me, the incident raised a serious consideration as to whether in our courts we are trying "behaviors" or the nonoperational "motives" we have been talking about.

Unfortunately, many of us still believe in witchcraft, and a significant example concerns mental illness.

"Illness" may be an inappropriate word, and in most cases I think it is. To me, a person is not "ill" or "sick" unless he has a structural illness, a known physical problem—an abscess, a lesion, bacteria, or a persistent biochemical imbalance.

In terms of those diagnosed as mentally ill, very few suffer from a structural illness.

Instead, they have a functional illness. They behave in ways unlike the ways of behaving practiced by others around them. The solution really is one of education, of helping the individual learn other ways of behaving, new options that will be more appropriate.

As a practicing psychologist, I have never liked the term "therapy" applied to what we typically do to help people cope with their lives. Indeed, on this basis I have never accepted third party payments (medical insurance) for my clients.

Readers of this book may wish to read the works of psychiatrist Thomas Szasz, especially *The Myth of Mental Illness* (New York, Dell, 1967) and *The Second Sin* (New York, Doubleday & Company, Inc., 1973).[1] In the latter book, Szasz writes that "mental illness is a myth whose function is to disguise and thus render more palatable the bitter pill of moral conflicts in human relations."

Szasz continues: "In asserting that there is no such thing as mental illness, I do not deny that people have problems coping with life and with each other."

People do experience difficulty relating to one another at times, and much of the difficulty, I think, comes from the fact that they have not learned options nor have they learned to accept responsibility for choosing the alternative which is most appropriate. Instead, they spend much of their time trying to figure out the *why*, the motivation. Interestingly enough, most of us tend to be more concerned with *why* when we are dealing with ineffective behavior. One isn't likely to say to his youngster, "Why *did* you make good grades?" But he predictably says, "Why *didn't* you make good grades?"

Try seeing your behavior and the behavior of others in terms of the Pull Concept. The behavior is to be understood not in terms of what caused it, but in terms of what it will elicit or avoid in the world when it occurs.

Behavior then can be seen as an *offense* mechanism

---

[1] Copyright 1973 by Thomas S. Szasz.

rather than a *defense* mechanism, the latter being a Freudian concept. A defense mechanism—such as compensation or identification—is traditionally explained as a way of "defending one's self" against the world. The shift I am suggesting here is from the Freudian "I'm helpless; I must defend myself" to my concept of behavior, "I'm taking the initiative to get something to happen."

The question we need to ask is "What do I want to happen after I have behaved in a particular way?"

And the next question is "What alternative ways of behaving are there which will produce more effective results for myself and for those with whom I am relating?"

six

The New "Language"

In this chapter I'd like you to look with me at interpersonal relationships, particularly at WHAT happens when two people relate rather than WHY it happens. My thinking here has been stimulated in part by the earlier works of Virginia Satir, such as *Conjoint Family Therapy* (Palo Alto, Science and Behavior Books, 1967) and *Peoplemaking* (Palo Alto, Science and Behavior Books, 1972).

Life is a series of interpersonal transactions between ourselves and the other persons in the world. I believe that most of us are taught three basic forms of behavior by which we conduct these transactions. We learn *to defer, to demand*, and *to defect*.

Deferring

Deferring behavior is learned at an early age when we are taught to do what other people expect us to do. We learn to please our parents and other authority figures by agreeing with them and by doing those things that will bring from them a positive response, or the avoidance of a negative one.

Even now, when I am deferring, I am giving up what I want to happen in deference to what *someone else* wants. I am canceling myself, at least for the moment.

Deferring Behavior   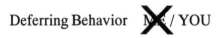ME / YOU

Demanding

At the same time we are taught to defer, we learn demanding behavior by imitating those who were telling us what to do and what to think about it. Consequently, we learn to demand specific behavior from other people.

When I am demanding, I am trying to get what I want by negating what *someone else* wants. I am asking the other person to cancel himself for me.

Demanding Behavior   ME / YOU

These two ways of behaving appear in dyadic relationships. Incidentally, I believe that relationships occur basically in dyads—that is, between two people at a time even if several are present. A child does not have a relationship with his parents. He has a unique one with his father and a unique one with his mother. Even in groups, formal or informal, I perceive relationships occurring in dyads. I do not see groups as having structures of their own—a group mind, for example—but rather as being composed of individuals functioning in relation to one another but nevertheless retaining their personal identity.

In most relationships, most of the time, one person is apparently demanding and the other deferring. This has been the basic relationship between parent and child, between teacher and student, between military officer and enlisted person, between employer and employee and between marriage partners. Within a relationship, a person may be deferring at times and demanding at other times. In fact, he may even take turns with his partner.

When both partners find a particular issue *significant* and they don't agree, the one who gets what he wants to happen may be perceived as the one successfully demanding. The one who submits, probably with some resentment, is the individual who is deferring.

When an issue is insignificant and one partner accepts the suggestion of another, this is *not* deferring.

When I was a child, deferring behavior seemed most appropriate. When I deferred, I was the "nice guy," the pleasant and obedient person who did what he was told as quickly and as quietly as possible. As I grew into adulthood, I continued my deferring behavior, agreeing with other people (superficially, at least) and determining what they thought about something before sticking out my own neck.

I discovered, however, that when I had done my nice thing for someone else, I suddenly shifted into a demanding mode, expecting the other person to come back with a "nice guy" response. In other words, I was attempting to get a positive response by deferring.

Defecting

The system worked, most of the time. But gradually I became aware that the system didn't always function as well as it had in earlier years. I didn't like being canceled out when I deferred, and I frequently said so by the way I behaved, usually employing the get-my-way behaviors discussed in Chapter 3.

The same thing sometimes happened when I demanded something of the other person and his response was not what I wanted. I was blocked again, and to get what I wanted, I employed one or more of those get-my-way techniques. When I used a get-my-way behavior, I was *defecting*, canceling both myself and the other person, at least temporarily.

I may have withdrawn or worried or slammed the door or shouted something such as "I'm leaving now, and I'm not coming back" or "I never want to see you again." Notice that what I am calling defecting behaviors are typically representative of the get-my-way "feelings" discussed earlier—helplessness, suffering, and anger.

So, the third way of behaving I had learned was defecting.

Defecting Behavior

Plotting it Out

Most everyone learns these three ways of interacting with other people in the world and, I believe, are usually *limited* in their learning to these three ways. The three behaviors—deferring, demanding, defecting—are not ego states nor do they represent types of people; they are *ways of behaving*. Most people are demanding in some situations with some people, deferring in other situations with other people, and at times defecting. What behavioral "position" I am in at any particular time is a matter of my own choosing.

I can *decide* how to behave, depending on what options I have learned. I think you have the same choice, depending on the options you have learned.

The options learned emerge largely from intimate relationships particularly within the family structure, the basic unit through which we learn how to relate to other people. And the primary relationship within the family is the marriage relationship, how the father and mother relate to one another.

My observation has been that in virtually all marriages there is a deferring-demanding relationship at the outset. Seldom are there two deferrers, because little would be accomplished. Picture such a couple in courtship.

"What do you want to do tonight?" the male asks.

"I don't care," his ladyfriend replies. "What do you want to do?"

"I don't have anything in mind, so let's do what you want to do," he says.

And so on until possibly one of the two says, "Well, I'll tell you what I expect to do." The deferring-deferring relationship has given way to deferring-demanding.

Just as seldom do two obvious demanders marry, because courtships involving such relationships tend not to lead to marriage unless there is complete agreement on what is demanded. When two demanders disagree, there is simply war (defecting) until one partner defers or the relationship dissolves.

In most marriages, at least at the beginning and perhaps for year after year, there is a deferring-demanding relationship and control is maintained by feelings.

Kurt Vonnegut, Jr., wrote in *Breakfast of Champions* of the machine-like quality of the people in these relationships, limited by the options they had learned:

> Your parents were fighting machines and self-pitying machines. Your mother was programmed to bawl out your father for being a defective money-making machine, and your father was programmed to bawl her out for being a defective housekeeping machine. They were programmed to bawl each other out for being defective loving machines. Then your father was programmed to stomp out of the house and slam the door. This automatically turned your mother into a weeping machine. And your father would go down to a tavern where he would get drunk with some other drinking machines. Then all the drinking machines would go to a whorehouse and rent *** machines. And then your father would drag himself home to become an apologizing machine. And your mother would become a very slow forgiving machine.[1]

Later in this chapter, I want to look more closely at what happens in marriage situations.

The point for now is that as with our *family* orientation, relationships outside the family take the same form, the deferring-demanding form, often resulting in defecting behavior.

In recent years, the deferring-demanding relationship has been challenged and modified. More demanding-demanding relationships seem to be common. For example, the traditional labor-management relationship had been deferring-demanding. With the rise of the labor movement during the last century, labor-management relationships

---

[1] Copyright 1973 by Kurt Vonnegut, Jr. Used with permission of Delacorte Press/ Seymour Lawrence and Jonathan Cape Ltd

have been increasingly characterized by demanding-demanding behavior, leading to some difficulty with eventual defecting behaviors, labeled strikes and lockouts.

More recently, women have demanded more equality, less "back of the bus" attitude from males. And on the college campus, especially since the 1960s, students have requested and sometimes demanded more say in administrative affairs. The new demanding-demanding relationship on the college campus has had a tremendous impact on "the changing university" in this and other countries.

Deferring-demanding behavior survives in interpersonal relationships because it works, at least for a time. As long as it is accepted by both parties, the deferring-demanding relationship appears to be a functioning one.

But, there may be problems.

The deferrer may grow tired of canceling himself out, and his first response may be to take the demanding "position":

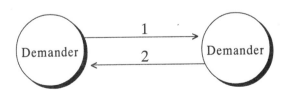

If that happens, the original demander may intensify his
position and seek to cancel his partner again:

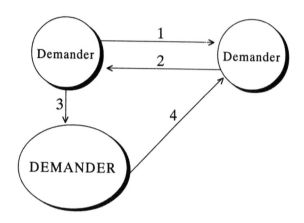

At this point, the deferrer working at demanding behavior may no longer be willing to accept his position, and he
may defect by becoming helpless, by suffering, or by
demonstrating anger.

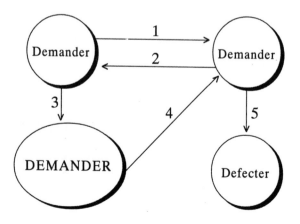

The demander now faced with a defector may also decide to defect, and the relationship crumbles:

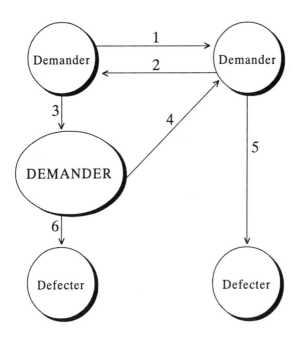

Such a situation is often seen in marriage counseling.

An example might be the couple married for several years, with the traditional deferring-demanding relationship in progress. The partner who seeks counseling first usually is the deferrer, who now has decided to withdraw (defect) in some fashion. The typical opening statement might sound like this: "I've had it. I'm through. That's enough."

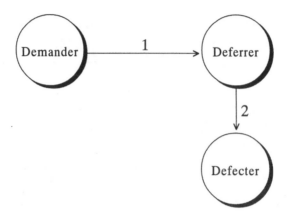

The demanding partner, in his first interview, is likely to report that "I just don't quite understand what's happened; I thought we had a perfect marriage," to which my reply would likely be "YOU probably did."

At any rate, the demanding partner—now unable to get his way directly—will be reduced to defecting:

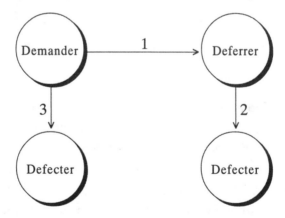

If the couple avoids divorce and recovers, the tendency will be to return to the original deferring-demanding relationship and "Act 2" of a continuing script begins.

Another alternative would be for the marriage partners to exchange roles. For example, the deferring spouse decides to become more assertive; to become the demander. This might, work for a while, but for how long could he continue without the previously in-charge partner developing resentment manifested in defecting?

The demander in any relationship is the individual who tries to get his way most of the time by canceling his partner and thereby remaining in control. But he can do that only as his deferring partner is willing to be canceled. In reality, then, the demander is quite brittle. If he ends up in a demanding-defecting relationship, he may himself elect the defecting position.

All three traditional ways of behaving . . .

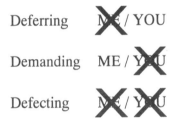

Deferring	M̶E̶ / YOU
Demanding	ME / Y̶O̶U̶
Defecting	M̶E̶ / Y̶O̶U̶

are self-oriented and designed to win. Actually, however, they are destined to lose. Viewed simply, they are a *win, lose* or *run away* set of options, but in each case at least one partner is immediately canceled. He loses. And because of that, in the long run, both will lose as relationship partners.

The deferrer appears to cancel himself out but in reality is attempting to control the other person by his deferring behavior and thereby elicit positive responses and avoid negative ones. He loses by apparently allowing his partner to get his way.

The deferrer most often is saying to himself internally, "I'm really *expected to* do so and so" or "I know I'm *supposed to* do such and such" or "I really *ought to* do this or that." And such internal sentences predictably are followed by the thought that "If I don't do what's expected, then my partner will give me some behavior I don't want"--helplessness, suffering, or anger. In this sense, then, the deferrer is accepting control by the other person by becoming responsible for the other's feelings, actual or assumed.

Demanders also are self-oriented, but more obviously. The demander's external pronouncements might sound this way: "You really *should* do such and such" or "You *ought* to do so and so" or "You're *expected* to do this or that." The demander is in control, at least for the moment. His control continues only as long as his partner agrees to respond in ways he has demanded.

Examples of deferring-demanding behavior are legion.

An easily understood example is that of a successful revolution, a situation in which there is deferring and demanding behavior heightened when the deferring people defect into rebellion. The deferrers first defect and then demand in order to defeat the present demanders. Such a situation requires that the previous demanders become deferrers if the revolution is to be successful. And, as you know from history, the new positions are tenuous at best, and another revolution is predictable, sooner or later.

I recall talking with a black gentleman one afternoon. We were discussing the racial issue in the United States, and I remember him saying that "change would have to come and come soon!"

I asked him what he wanted to happen, specifically.

"Well," he said, "we blacks want to be on top like you whites have always been."

As we talked, we agreed that historically the whites in this country had been the demanders and the blacks had been the deferrers. We also agreed that the relationship had not be effective or appropriate. The blacks resented canceling themselves out; they wanted to win but found they were continually losing.

As my friend suggested, the blacks wanted a change in roles. They wanted to exchange places with the whites in terms of their behavior. They wanted to become demanders and invite the whites to become deferrers. We both could recall several instances in history when oppressed peoples attempted change by becoming demanders through violent acts of defection. None produced lasting positive results.

We also agreed that a shift in roles between blacks and whites would not likely accomplish much at all. No long-lasting improvement would result because the whites would no more want to lose than had the blacks. Similar resentment would occur predictably and understandably.

I suggested that another option was needed, an option that would force neither blacks nor whites into a win, lose, or run away position.

What would the new option be?

I believe a new option would have helped in the Vietnam conflict. In Southeast Asia in the late 1960s and early 1970s, the United States found that it didn't want to lose, apparently could not or would not win, and would suffer embarrassment by running away. So we just sat there! A new option might have offered a more appropriate alternative.

Most of us experience the same win-lose-or run away alternatives in our encounters with other people.

We learn as youngsters to defer at times so that we can have and keep friends. "Play nice," parents say, "or your friends won't come back again. They won't like you anymore." We counterfeit ourselves: we cancel ourselves in deference to our playmates, but we don't like to do it.

At times, we may have decided to be demanders in our childhood relationships, canceling our friends, who probably didn't relate with us that way for very long. In either case, we might have ended up as defectors, and thereby canceling the entire relationship.

Another option would have been valuable to us then also.

I see many examples of deferring, demanding, and defecting behaviors on the college campus. Consider the fraternity or sorority system, a classic win-lose-run away situation. As pledges, young people behave in the deferring fashion. Later, their deference (which they endure but seldom enjoy) comes to an end when they are admitted to active membership in the organization. Then, these one-time deferrers shift into demanding behavior as actives, eager to attract a new pledge class composed of prospective brothers or sisters who will be asked to use deferring behavior.

Occasionally, a pledge will tire of canceling himself and

defect. He may withdraw, become "angry" or verbally attack.

College roommates experience a similar relationship at times. A typical situation occurs when one roommate wants to study in quiet surroundings, but his partner prefers loud music at the same time. One of the two predictably will demand and the other will defer.

The deferring person, probably the student who enjoys quiet, may go to the library. For a while that may solve the problem but eventually he will grow bored with being canceled and may decide to defect, inviting anything from argument to quarrel, the search for a new roommate, or perhaps a change in roles as the deferrer becomes the demander, the demander moves into deferring behavior, and the cycle continues ploddingly through the school year.

They might have found another option to be more productive.

As I've said before in this chapter, deferring, demanding, and defecting behaviors involve cancellation. In deferring, I cancel myself. In demanding, I seek to cancel the other person. In defecting, both myself and the other person are canceled, at least temporarily in the relationship.

Even when one person is canceled, as in deferring and demanding behavior, both persons eventually are canceled, both lose in the long run.

Now, before you continue reading, I'd like to invite you to consider one or two relationships in which you are involved at the moment. Project them over a period of time.

You might select your relationship with your husband or wife, boyfriend or girlfriend, employer or a parent.

Can you see who *you* are in the relationship?

Would you like a new option to the ways you have been behaving, an option in which no one was canceled, or at least not entirely?

Do you think that's possible?

I do.

Declaring

I believe there is a new option. It simply must be learned as an alternative to deferring, demanding, and defecting, the three traditional ways of behaving in interpersonal relationships.

The new system or option is a fourth "language" of behavior. It is quite simple but seldom taught in our culture. I am convinced that most of the problems people experience in interpersonal relationships are the result of restricted options. My suggestion, then, is, as I've said in a previous chapter, that these people are not "ill" and requiring therapy, but rather that they need to learn a new alternative or "language."

Consider in analogy a person who had learned to speak English, French, and German. Suppose he were to find himself suddenly transported to a Russian village where no one spoke anything but Russian. Since he spoke no Russian, he would have difficulty conducting business with the natives. He couldn't converse with them nor could he immediately establish any significant relationships. This person could be termed maladjusted, but not ill. He did not need therapy; he wasn't sick. He simply needed to learn the Russian language.

So it is with the fourth option in relationships, a new language of conducting interpersonal processes with other people in dyads.

The new option is one I call *declaring*. No one in the dyad--not ME, not YOU--is canceled.

Declaring Behavior   ME / YOU

When I am declaring, I am speaking in the *first person singular*. I am making *declarative* statements about what I want to happen, using *operational definitions*. I am dealing with *issues* based upon *data* I have collected. I am willing to *negotiate*.

The fourth language may strike you as simplistic. It certainly is simple. Nearly anyone can learn it and use it, if he decides to add it to his repertoire.

In declaring, I am simply saying what I want to happen, rather than demanding that it happen, or deferring to the wants of the other person. And I invite my dyad partner to declare his wishes too.

Negotiation vs. Compromise

Once we have both made our declarations, we may negotiate any differences. "Negotiation" is a key word here, and one I want to comment on at greater length.

The traditional deferring-demanding relationship often leads to compromise conditions, whereas the declaring-declaring relationship often includes negotiation. Compromise and negotiation are not the same, although at first glance they may appear to be similar.

Operationally defined, compromise might mean something such as "If you let me win this time, I'll let you win
next time." The problem with compromise is that both
parties are forced to keep books on whose turn it is to win,
and no one is quite as good a bookkeeper as his partner
would want him to be.

In negotiation, both parties deal with issues rather than
with feelings, and with data collected regarding the issues.
In negotiation, there is no residue, no owing anybody later,
no keeping of books as to who gave in to whom and when.
Instead of dealing with feelings, the person who is declaring
is oriented to issues. He is responsive to the shared situation.

Saying this another way:

* When a person is blocked, he traditionally presents
  feelings, asking others to be responsible for them.
  These are the get-my-way tools of Chapter 3, represented here as defecting behavior.

* The new language or option is to deal not with
  feelings, but with issues based upon data collected.

* As the declaring person, I evaluate the data and then
  declare what I want to happen, not what I want the
  other person to do. I recognize that I alone am responsible for my own behavior.

* I talk in first person singular about what I want, and I
  use operational terms.

The four ways of conducting transactions with other
people may be clearer with one or two examples. Look with
me at a married couple who decided not to eat at home one
evening.

They collect data. The husband wants to eat Italian food,

the wife wants Danish food.

They collect more data. No restaurant in the area serves both kinds of food, but there are restaurants specializing in Danish and in Italian food.

How would these partners function in the various ways of relating discussed in this chapter?

If they have a deferring-demanding relationship, the most common in marriages, the decision probably will be made that the deferrer will agree to go the demander's restaurant. In this case, let's suppose that the man is the deferrer and his wife, the demander.

Apparently, then, the wife is winning. She's getting her way:

Suppose further that the husband is driving the car. He's the deferrer, remember. As the car approaches the Danish restaurant, the husband with a sigh in his voice might say, "There's no place to park at this restaurant" or "Look how small the parking spaces are" or "There are too many people here already; we'll have to stand in line."

Later, he may announce, "There's nothing on the menu I really want to eat." He may talk about the "lousy service" or the "cold food." And to cap his pronouncements: "Well, I hope you're happy here." (Suffer, suffer, suffer!)

The husband has chosen his defecting behavior:

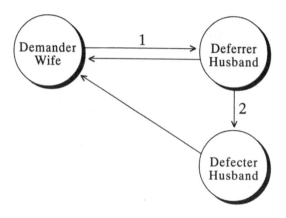

At the beginning of this transaction, the deferring husband was canceled. As he begins to defect, the demander-wife--faced with her husband's defecting behavior--may find herself at a dinner conducted in an atmosphere of attack by suffering. Both partners lose. The wife was winning by being in her restaurant, but she is losing in the relationship just as is the husband from the outset.

What might happen if two defectors were in this situation? What would they do?

They would compromise and perhaps go to a Chinese restaurant. They would both lose immediately. Neither is getting what he wants, and both are saying, at least internally, "If I can't have my way, you're not going to have your way either, so there!"

Their record books will reflect that decision for the future.

These are traditional and easily recognizable reactions to a rather common situation. Remember, too, that problems exist between deferring-demanding partners and defecting-defecting partners only in those circumstances where the issue is important to both and they don't agree.

Now test your understanding of the new system, the *declaring* transaction in which no one loses entirely. In this specific case both husband and wife will deal with the issue rather than with feelings, and there will be no residue because there will be no compromise.

Consider what will happen in this *declaring* transaction before you continue reading. You might ask someone to help you plot out the transaction in a role-playing situation.

Both of you will be declaring in first-person-singular sentences using operational terms. You will be dealing with the following data: the partners have agreed to eat away from home; they do not want to take food home for that is not eating out; and each of the partners prefers a different type of food not available in any single restaurant. The issue here is specific food away from home.

What would the declarer do so as to cancel no one?

If you have difficulty, consider some of the additional *assumptions* which may not be part of the collected data.

Are you considering, for example, that the couple *must* eat *together*?

That isn't part of our data, yet. Nothing dictates that the partners must go to the same restaurant. Remember, the issue here is food, not "Do you love me?"

They *could* eat in separate restaurants, she going to the Danish restaurant and he to the Italian. You might react negatively to this suggestion, and if you do, perhaps you are dealing with feelings rather than with the situation. On what basis should we assume that the husband and wife *must* eat together? They probably didn't eat lunch together.

Certainly there's nothing undesirable about them *wanting* to be together for dinner, so let's complicate the matter by adding in the desire of each partner to dine with the other as well as to have the kind of food each desires.

Given these data, what can the declaring-declaring couple now do?

Do some more thinking before you read on.

If you have further difficulty in resolving this, perhaps you are making another *assumption*: that the husband and wife *must* eat at the *same* time. By dropping this assumption, again there is no problem. The two can go successively to both restaurants. No one loses. They are together and each has the food he or she wishes.

But now, whose restaurant would they go to first?

More data must be collected? Who had the late lunch? Where are the restaurants located? What are the serving hours?

More decisions can be made based on the data additionally collected and evaluated.

The point is that the declaring couple collects all the relevant information possible and then negotiates a decision. No defecting-type feelings are involved. No nonoperational language is used. And no one loses entirely. In fact, they both can win.

In declaring relationships, another significant factor that must be considered is what I call the hierarchy of wants or wishes.

Declaring people have such a hierarchy. Not all their wants must be fulfilled. When a person is a declarer, he is free to decide the relative strength of his wants, and he may decide to forgo one or more of them to achieve another.

In the restaurant example, suppose that one spouse has only an hour available for dinner because of an evening engagement. He may decide, then, that his wish to be together with the other is--for him--more important than is his wish for a particular food. He decides to eat with his spouse in the restaurant of his/her choice, forgoing his other wishes as being farther down his hierarchy. It is *his* decision for *his* wishes, thus the spouse "owes" him nothing for going to his/her restaurant.

Some readers may see this decision as deferring behavior, but I do not. Deferring behavior is designed to prevent unwanted behavior from a partner or internally from oneself. In the example I've just described, this spouse simply is selecting his wishes for his own purposes and to his own best fulfillment.

The declarer does not *have* to win. He simply declares his own wants or wishes and determines how he can best go about fulfilling those wants in his hierarchical scale. He does this by being *responsive* to the total shared situation, including the other person's wishes, yet not being responsible for the other person's feelings.

A friend of mine stopped by my office.

"I've got a problem," he said after a while. "My wife is never on time for anything. She's always late. No matter where we go, we get there after everything's started."

"How long has this been going on?" I asked.

"Ever since we were married, I guess. About eighteen years."

"On what basis are *you* late?" I asked him.

"It's not me. I've already told you. It's my wife who's always late."

"Yes, but what keeps *you* from being on time? You have two cars, don't you? *You* could be on time, and your wife could join you later."

He paused. "No, I couldn't do that. I couldn't go without her. She'd be upset."

"But you've been upset for eighteen years, haven't you?"

My friend, a deferring person in this transaction, had been the nice guy. He had been canceling himself, but then he would manifest defecting behavior. After each social event to which he and his wife had arrived late, a day or two of "recovery" had been necessary.

I suggested to him that he might try *declaring* his wants. By doing that, I said, neither he nor his wife would have to lose entirely. He could be on time, if he wished. His wife could be late, if she wished.

Later, he told me what happened the next time he and his wife were preparing for an evening engagement.

"Jane," he had said, "the party is at eight o'clock, and I'd like to go on time tonight. I'm planning on leaving at seven forty-five. I would like to go to the party with you. I'm available to help you in any way that will assist you in being able to leave with me."

That particular time, he reported, his wife was not ready to leave at 7:45, and so he left for the party alone. She joined him there later.

"Your wife had the prerogative to go late if she wanted to," I said.

"Yes," he replied.

"And you had the prerogative to be on time if you wanted to."

"Of course."

My friend went on to explain that recently he and his wife had been going to social events on time, together. What had happened was that his wife had decided that she would rather go *with* her husband on time than go *without* her husband late, although she had both options available to her. She changed her behavior in response to her husband changing his. Previously she had not had to consider her own hierarchy of wishes.

In declaring, a person states what he wishes or wants to happen. There are no expectations, no dealings with feelings. Instead, there is self-responsible behavior that directly concerns issues, the situation.

I gave a talk one afternoon to a group. After my speech, a person approached me and (in a demanding transaction) said, "Well, you certainly stepped on my toes with your remarks."

If I had responded in a deferring way in this transaction, how would I have behaved?

I could have said something such as, "Oh, I'm so sorry. I apologize." To which the person might have replied (in a demanding way): "Okay, but don't do it again."

I might have elected to reply in a demanding way. My response then might have sounded this way: "No, I didn't, and besides, the fee wasn't large enough to stand out here and take this from you." such a remark probably would have led to an additional verbal skirmish.

Or perhaps as a defector: "I can't talk with you about it right now; I have an appointment. I must go."

But I elected a *declaring* response and said: "I appreciate you telling me what you think. Thank you for the feedback." I could have responded in numerous declaring ways.

In this instance, I neither lost nor attempted to win, nor did I run away. The confrontation was disarmed.

And in a very few moments, in the same small group in which we had been chatting, this particular person and I were talking and smiling again.

As you have perhaps seen, the declaring response is "disarming" rather than "defeating." That's an important distinction between declaring behavior as opposed to the more traditional ways of relating, deferring-demanding-defecting.

Again, you might take time to review some of your ongoing relationships. Plot them out and determine how they might be different if declaring behavior were used.

Readers of this book will, I hope, have little difficulty recognizing the four ways of behaving. There are many cues, given both in actions and words, that can help us decide the "position" of a partner in a relationship.

Nonverbal language can also be significant. The deferring person often assumes the body language and gestures of the young child. Eye contact may be slight, seldom direct. The voice may have a "pleading" quality, may sound apologetic. The demanding person may appear more authoritarian. He may point a finger or stand with hands on hips. Eye contact may be longer, more direct. Some demanders may appear quite differently, however. They may come on quietly, almost as deferrers. The demanding person is not necessarily the most verbal one; he's simply the person who gets his way as his partner defers. Demanders have intense expectations and are quite brittle when faced with even polite rebuttal.

Finally, the declaring person, in addition to his first-person-singular operational-definition approach, may demonstrate his declaring "position" by direct eye-level contact.

A last point in this chapter.

In declaring behavior, the declarer states his wishes and may negotiate. But some wishes are extremely significant and nonnegotiable. When this happens, the two people involved may decide that the cost of the relationship is too great, either on a particular issue or in total.

An example of this might concern a young couple married a few years. The husband declares that he would like to have two children in the next four years. The wife declares that she wants no children at all. The issue is drawn, and data must be collected. The husband attempts to negotiate, suggesting that if the wife is afraid of pregnancy, they might adopt children. The wife replies that she is not afraid of pregnancy, that she simply does not want any children. Eventually, they conclude that they have a nonnegotiable set of wishes.

Whether this couple has children or not, one of them loses immediately, and ultimately both will lose.

In a situation of nonnegotiable wishes, there is the likelihood that staying together may cost each of the partners much too much. They may then elect to dissolve the relationship.

They agree to withdraw from one another as the most appropriate response to the shared situation. Neither is expecting or anticipating the other to change *his* "position" to prevent the withdrawal.

Some readers may have difficulty accepting the issue-oriented concept I am proposing in this book because our society is so highly power-structured. There are countless examples of demand situations in which "the other side" is expected to defer and often does. This happens in political and social circles, in business, and within academic relationships.

While preparing this chapter, I heard a radio commentator quoting the economist Jean Monnet. The quote seemed illustrative of the issue-oriented concept I have been recommending.

Monnet had suggested that rather than two individuals or nations confronting one another across the table, it would be preferable for the two to share the same side of the table, confronting the problem on the other side.

There are, in fact, very few really nonnegotiable situations.

seven

Using the New "Language"

The Me(s) in We

Chris Smith is thirty-nine, a computer consultant in a nearby city. Chris and his wife Lucille, a CPA, live in a suburban home with their son, Steve, age five.

Both Chris and Lucille understand and practice the declaring option.

The Smiths are on-the-go people. Chris is a member of several clubs and civic organizations, and the coach of a Little League baseball team. Lucille has been spending many evenings at the community's service center for the elderly.

When the Smiths were married six years ago, they agreed that at least one night a week would be reserved for something they wanted to do together. So, on almost every Friday evening, Chris and Lucille take in a movie, visit with friends, host a party, or drive to a nearby lake where Chris is building a small cabin on five acres of land purchased a year ago.

Tonight is Tuesday night. The dinner dishes have been

done. Lucille is reading the newspaper, and Chris is preparing to leave for Little League practice at seven o'clock.

"Chris," Lucille says, "I'd like to see the play at the Community Theater Friday night."

Lucille has spoken a declarative sentence. In first person singular, she has declared what she wants to happen.

"I don't especially want to see the play," Chris replies.

Another first-person-singular declarative sentence.

Underway in the Smith home at this particular moment is a declarer-declarer relationship but without agreement.

"Is the play on another night?" Chris asks.

"Yes. It's on Thursday night."

"I have Jaycees Thursday night. Perhaps you might see the play then," Chris says.

This conversation is an example of the new declaring option. The negotiating phase, identifying the issue and collecting data, is in progress between two adults who are self-responsible and operational. If Lucille sees the play Thursday night by herself or with a friend, then the issue is seeing the play and not her husband taking her to the theater performance. She would be available to spend Friday evening with Chris doing something they both might wish to do.

Suppose, however, that the Community Theater is a one-night production, and so the play is presented Friday night only. What then?

Chris might decide to attend the play with her.

Would that mean he was deferring to her?

Not necessarily.

He would have been a deferrer had he said to himself, "I

suppose I ought to take her to the play Friday night or she'll be upset for the whole weekend."

Remember that the deferrer is controlled by the other person's expressed or potential feelings.

Chris, as a declarer, instead looks at his own hierarchy of wishes. He apparently doesn't have anything in mind that he wants to do Friday night other than be with his wife. He can forgo his lack of interest about the play in order to fulfill his wish to be with her. Or, assuming that the play will also be performed on Thursday evening, by Lucille's attending the play then and being with her husband and doing something they both wish to do on Friday evening, nobody in the relationship loses at all.

Incidentally, had Chris been a defector, he would have claimed some kind of helplessness or demonstrated suffering or anger when the play was suggested. Then, had Lucille been demanding, she might have slipped into defecting with some get-my-way behavior of her own.

What do you think might have taken place at the outset of this example had Lucille not been a declarer?

Let's imagine her as a deferring wife.

"Chris," Lucille says, "would it be okay if we see a play Friday night, down at the Community Theater?"

Or she might have said something such as: "Chris, would you be interested in seeing a play Friday night?"

Notice the absence of any declarative statement expressing what the speaker wants to happen. Neither is there any first person singular. The deferrer declares only by inference. The question approach automatically puts the other person in charge.

As a result, if the deferrer doesn't get what she wants, she is protected. She really hasn't put herself on the line by saying what she wants to do.

Chris probably will answer his wife's question. Can you play the dialogue through to see what might take place, assigning Chris any one of the several options?

Now, suppose Lucille were a demander. In this case, she undoubtedly would speak in a second or third person, followed by "ought," "should," "supposed to," "must," "expected," or a similar word.

"Chris"--Lucille looks across the room at him--"we haven't been to a play in a long time. We ought to go Friday night. You pick up the tickets tomorrow when you're downtown."

Again, try playing through the dialogue to see what might happen between Chris and Lucille.

Finally, suppose that Lucille is a defecting wife. The Tuesday night scene might go something like this.

Lucille, reading the paper, suddenly sighs...a long and audible "suffering" sigh.

"What's wrong?" Chris asks (now impaled on Lucille's hook-sigh).

"Oh, nothing."

"Something must be the matter. I heard you sigh, Lucille. What's wrong? What's the matter? Tell me," Chris says (now really hooked).

"Oh, you wouldn't go anyway," Lucille says.

"I might. Where do you want to go? Tell me, and we'll go," Chris says.

"To a play Friday night at the Community Theater,"

Lucille delivers the blow quickly but surely.

And so on through the dialogue.

Fortunately, the Smiths do not ask each other to lose.

The Wish List

When Chris and Lucille were married soon after graduation from college, I suggested that they complete what I call a "wish list," an exercise for couples who want a relationship without helplessness, suffering, or anger. The wish list can be adapted rather easily for any dyad relationship.

In discussing the wish list with them, I suggested that an operational definition of marriage might sound something like this: marriage is two people agreeing to conduct life together in ways they both like.

When Chris and Lucille began their wish list, I asked them to agree first on the major categories of life that a married couple conduct together. Such categories usually would include money, sex, socializing, religion, in-laws, children, careers, food, housing and recreation.

After they agreed on about ten categories, I asked each of them to write in detail his or her wishes for each category. Each item was to be in first person singular and expressed operationally.

This was not to be, I emphasized, a list of feelings. Rather, I wanted each person to say what he or she wanted to happen.

Nor was it to be a "gripe list," what each person in the relationship wanted the other to do. Instead, the wish list was to center on what each person wanted to have happen in his or her own life. That might, of course, include implications for the other person.

Finally, I said, they were not to share their lists with each other just yet.

After several days of editing and rewriting, they returned with their individual lists, and we reviewed them separately. Some feelings had crept in and one or two abstractions were used instead of operational definitions.

Chris and Lucille took their lists home again to do more work.

Finally, the two wish lists were ready.

As an example, here were Lucille's notations under religion:

* I would like to be a member of a Protestant church, preferably Lutheran.
* I would like the church to be in our neighborhood.
* I would like to attend church two out of four Sundays each month.
* I would like to participate in one additional function of the church.
* I would like to participate in appropriate functions of the church with my husband.

Next, I asked them to agree on a time to hear each other's list and to attempt negotiation. Negotiation would involve issues and data, not feelings. The time set aside would be one when there would be little distraction.

I also suggested that they employ a recorder to tape their discussion. The best procedure, I explained, was this:

   a. record the discussion of wishes and negotiation,

   b. later, listen to the recording without comment or

discussion. This could be done individually or together, and

c. record a second discussion regarding reactions to the
original recording.

Chris and Lucille each knew how the other sounded and
operated in discussion but, like most of us, neither was
probably much aware of the process and voice intonation
he or she used. The original tape recording quite often
points up get-my-way techniques of which one or both
partners are unaware.

The point to this exercise between partners is to clarify
wishes and to find ways to negotiate those wishes. (Review
the difference between negotiation and compromise in
Chapter 6.)

Sometimes a partner will have to forgo a wish if, in the
hierarchy of wishes, another seems more appropriate.

And sometimes, although not often, the couple will
have to decide whether or not the price of the relationship
is too high.

Chris and Lucille discovered several wishes one or the
other would have to forgo. They discussed and found ways
to negotiate those differences. They did not find any
nonnegotiable wishes.

The wish-list exercise requires time and careful thought.
But I believe the energy expended is a worthy investment.
It can make clear at an early stage, even before marriage,
whether the relationship has a chance to survive.

The list can be modified whenever change seems
necessary.

The wish list also works quite well in relationships

between parents and teen-age sons or daughters. Once the lists are completed and negotiations carried out, both of the parents (a wish list for each) and their offspring (a separate list for each) know infinitely more about establishing worthwhile relationships without the ineffective after effects of get-my-way behaviors.

How it Works

The new option of declaring is very effective with young people who are exploring their own individual concept of freedom from about the age of fourteen or fifteen. I appreciate William Allen White's definition of freedom. White suggested that freedom is the one thing you can't have unless you give it away. Both people in a relationship must be free.

Freedom does not mean that each person can do whatever he wants to do. There are too many people for that. If each person did exactly what he pleased, we would experience total chaos to the point that no one would have any freedom at all.

The declaring option recognizes each person's right to be who he is and to accept the consequences of his behavior. And it also recognizes that he must relate to other people if he is to survive. Freedom, then, is a matter of seeing alternatives clearly and making worthwhile decisions based on those alternatives.

So far in this chapter, I have been exploring the marriage relationship in terms of the four languages of behavior. Let's look at some other kinds of dyad transactions.

Consider the hard-sell demanding salesperson who must

have a deferring customer if his sales techniques are to be successful. His deferring customer may very well accept the sale in order to rid himself of the salesperson. But I've discovered that this type of salesperson may not be as successful as he might appear to be at first glance. The deferring customer quite likely may defect--hours or days later--and cancel the order. Several states have enacted laws that allow a harassed customer of this type to cancel contracts within three to seven days. Such protection may indeed be desirable for deferrers who are unable to handle demander-salespersons.

What kind of salesperson would you wish to approach you in a store or in your home? Do you prefer one who shares data, or one who operates on your feelings?

In dealing with an insurance salesperson, how do you respond to one who attempts to develop guilt feelings in you rather than one who shares with you rational data regarding your family needs?

Still another typical situation which illustrates the languages of behavior is the employer-employee transaction.

As an employer, would you like to have a deferring employee (the typical yes-person), or would you want an employee who provided you with declarative data?

A few years ago, a young lady employed in my office asked to speak with me in private.

"Would you be upset if I took another job?" she asked.

"Well, I really don't like the options you've given me," I replied.

She didn't seem to understand my response, and so I explained.

"If I get upset, you hint you'll probably stay, but perhaps with some resentment. If I don't get upset, I can only infer that you will take the other job. I don't like the options. But, more importantly, I don't want to make your decision for you."

She understood a little more clearly what I was saying, and so she tried again.

"Should I leave here, would it present extreme difficulties for you?" she asked.

My reply was this: "If you stay, that will be fine. If you leave, I can handle it. I'd like for you to make your own decision based on the data which is significant for you. I do appreciate you considering my situation."

The next morning, she announced that she had elected to remain in my office.

The declaring person--the self-responsible person--decides to respond to the shared situation. He does not attempt to be responsible for the other person's feelings.

Helping young people understand the declaring option can begin early in their lives.

One person told me such an experience with his seven-year-old daughter.

He said that he had scolded her one day for something she had done. The scolding, he realized almost immediately, was inappropriate for the child's behavior. The daughter, Anne, ran to her room, closed the door, and began to cry.

Ed, my client, understood that if he went to her as she continued to cry, he would only reinforce the crying response to such situations. So he waited until Anne stopped crying. Then he went to her room.

He told her that he had not liked what he had done when he scolded her, that her behavior had not deserved such a reaction from him and that he wanted her to know that. He held her close.

Ed was teaching Anne the new language of behavior, an option he wanted Anne to learn to use. He was teaching by example, taking responsibility for his own actions and doing so in first person singular.

This incident is another example of the Pull Theory discussed in Chapter 5.

Note that Ed did not apologize. He did not say he was "sorry."

There are two kinds of apologies. There's the ritualistic apology that occurs whenever we bump into someone or we sneeze. And there's the second kind of apology that is involved in more crucial interpersonal relationships. This second type of apology is fraudulent. Saying "I'm sorry" places the other partner in a type of psychological double jeopardy. Not only was he subjected to the inappropriate behavior, he is also being asked to forgive and, in effect, give permission for it to occur again.

An apology in these significant interpersonal relationships amounts to manipulation. Actually, if you did regret the event and not the response from the other person, you could have decided not to do whatever you did in the first place.

I propose in such an apology situation that instead of saying "I'm sorry," one might say something such as "I'd like you to know that I am aware my behavior was not appropriate (or worthwhile), and I intend to work at changing it for the future."

Under the new option of declaring, I tell the offended party that I recognize my own inadequate behavior, which is mine alone. I make no requirement or demand that I be forgiven.

Which brings us back to the central issue of this book.

I believe that most people have been trained to believe that *someone else* decides whether or not they are worthwhile. When we were young, the "someone else" was our parents and other authority figures, who said such things as "If you really loved me, you would do this or that." We were worthwhile if we did what we were *supposed* to do.

School teachers later assumed the role of parents, and still later the role was played by members of our peer group. All along, someone else decided whether or not we really were worthy, or at least we gave them that prerogative.

The Bible points this out in an interesting way to me. I perceive the Old Testament as being basically an authoritarian model. Fulfill the law, the Old Testament demands: thou shalt not kill, thou shalt not steal, thou shalt not commit adultery.

The New Testament, on the other hand, speaks to me more in the new option of declaring. The new commandment was to love others as yourself. There was no period or comma after others. Neither the other nor you were to be canceled. Also, the individual has volition. He is *free* to decide what behavior is appropriate and worthwhile for him. The New Testament orientation is that it's *not appropriate* to kill or steal or commit adultery, but one may decide otherwise, accepting responsibility for the consequences likely to follow.

The Good Samaritan did what was *appropriate*, not what was required under the law. He saw the issue, and he collected and evaluated data. He determined, on the basis of his evidence, that the most worthwhile act was to care for the stranger, which he did.

Christ, in approaching the crowd and the woman about to be stoned, did what was appropriate and worthwhile, not because the law demanded that he act in that certain way.

Notice again and again two significant words: "appropriate," "worthwhile."

The self-responsible person does what he does out of a sense of appropriateness and worthwhileness.

He stops at a stop sign when he is driving his car not because he is deferring, but because the stop is appropriate. Someone has collected data and determined that cars need to stop at this particular location. In order to guarantee freedom to all drivers, some cars stop while others continue. Then, the order is reversed. Freedom, we recall White saying, is the one thing you can't have unless you give it away.

The self-responsible person deals with the issue, the shared situation, and then matches appropriate behavior to it.

And there's a significant difference between doing something that seems appropriate or worthwhile and doing something so as not to get caught. One must ask himself: Is my behavior appropriate, or am I doing this because I think I can get away with it? If the latter, the person really is claiming that if he doesn't upset anybody, it's okay to do what he's doing. Again, you see, he's not under his own control. Someone else has his box of "buttons."

College students often come to discuss choosing a major field of study. One such conversation began this way: "I want to major in art, but Dad says I should major in business, and if I don't, he won't pay the tuition."

"I'll ask you a question," I begin. "Are you prepared to do without your father's money? Will you put yourself through school, working part time, and perhaps taking a little longer to get your degree in art?"

I point out that his life and what he does with it are his, but his father's money is his father's.

If the student concludes that he is prepared to obtain his education on his own, then I suggest that when he returns home, he might declare in first person singular that he wishes to major in art.

If his father counters by announcing he will stop tuition payments, then the son might say something such as: "All right, Dad, I understand that the money is yours and you may use it as you wish, in whatever way is appropriate for you. I'm prepared to handle the situation by spending a few more months in school and by working part time to pay my tuition. I think that is appropriate for me because I wish to major in art. We are both doing what we think is worthwhile."

This isn't defecting. It is *disarming*.

When the student decides to be in charge of himself, there is no war. but there may be no agreement either. The student isn't angry or hurt. He is handling the situation, including the possible consequences.

When the father's get-my-way tool (money) is disarmed, the father eventually will recover. He still may not pay the tuition.

In the several cases in which a similar experience has been reported, not a single father withdrew the tuition money although each of them could have.

Recall a statement that I made in Chapter 2. When one person changes his behavior, he invites others around him to change their behavior also.

In any relationship, each of the partners has the prerogative to behave either effectively or ineffectively. If the other person decides to be ineffective, there is no requirement that I must adopt similar ineffective ways of behaving. How I decide to behave is my choice.

When one person behaves consistently as a declarer, others in relationship find it difficult to maintain any of the deferring, demanding, or defecting positions.

A friend of mine once received a telephone call from his eighteen-year-old son. The son was calling from a college campus seventy-five miles away, at eleven thirty at night.

"Dad," he began, "I'm at the college and I've been visiting with Gene. May I stay overnight?"

The father had learned how to be a declarer and had been trying to help his son learn the new language also.

"I am wondering if you want me to be parental?" the father asked.

"Come on," John said, "cut that stuff out. Can I stay?"

"I'd like some data, John," the father said. "For a start, where do you intend to stay overnight?"

"In one of the dormitories."

"Have you made arrangements?"

"No, not yet. But I will."

"If you can't stay there, where will you stay? Have you money for a motel?"

"No."

"Then where will you stay?"

"Well, I could sleep in the car."

"I wish you wouldn't do that, John. I really don't believe you are fully prepared to stay there for the night, and I wish you would come home. However, if you aren't home by two o'clock, I'll assume you are staying overnight."

That was the end of the call. No voodoo concept was in operation; there were no deferring, demanding, or defecting behaviors on the father's part.

At a quarter of two, my friend said, John arrived home.

The next morning, the father explained the declaring language in greater detail to his son, telling him how he would have liked the situation handled in a way that would be beneficial to both of them.

A few weeks later, John again was visiting Gene on the college campus.

Another phone call. But this time, John used the new system he was learning.

"Dad, this is John. I'm planning to stay overnight. I've made arrangements with Mr. Swift to sleep in the dorm, and I have the ten-dollar overnight fee. I'll be home by noon tomorrow. I wanted you to know what my plans were, and I'm wondering if it would be convenient for me to keep the car until noon when I get back."

The previous conversation had begun with a deferring

question. The second call opened with a declaration.

In the second call, John was declaring his plans and was sharing the data he had collected. John's father still had the prerogative to suggest data that his son might have overlooked, or he could express appreciation for the call, a further reinforcement of the new declaring option.

When young adults and their parents both learn and use the new language of behavior, many of the ineffective situations associated with "growing up" are avoided.

The transition from child to adolescent to young adult is a difficult and curious one in our culture. There are few pubertal rites, for example, few ways that an individual can show he has reached adulthood. With the possible exception of receiving a driver's license, there is almost no standard and culturally acceptable procedure in our society as a whole to mark the passage from childhood to adulthood.

So how do young people demonstrate that they are becoming adult?

Frequently they do so by doing those things off-limits to them but open to older adults. I have in mind such things as smoking, drinking, being involved with drugs and sex, and other actions that tend to be exciting ways of demonstrating their independence.

Young people want to establish themselves as adults, and they often do so at the expense of their parents' wishes and, sometimes, their demands.

Up to about twelve years of age, an individual is part of a parent-child culture. A youngster is taught to defer to the demanding parent.

At the same time he learns to be responsible for other

people's feelings, as I have suggested in this book. Then, at about twelve or thirteen, his "need to please" shifts from his parents to his peer group, and there usually emerges a kind of "peer group parent" to which he demonstrates allegiance. The young adult is fairly certain that his parents will continue to be interested in him, but he may not be so sure of his peer group. He looks for ways to tie himself to his peers, and his peers to himself.

To his parents, his activity may appear to be defecting behavior. In effect, he says to them, "I don't really want to do what you want me to do." He becomes a "rebel," which may be defined operationally as a person who is not doing what someone else expects him to do.

Parents often see the issue as one of "character," but I see it as the case of a young person replacing one demander (his real parent) with another (his peer group parent). The new demander can be an individual, a popular movement, an attractive philosophical statement, any one of the several sub-groups in the typical school, the neighborhood gang or anything to which he decides to defer.

The young person himself may not perceive this at first. He usually sees himself as an independent thinker, a "free" person. Essentially, however, he is rebelling against the original parent but deferring to the new one. He is doing what he has been taught to do.

In class one afternoon, I encountered a student who had grown a mustache, the style of the day. The student insisted that in no way had the growing of the mustache been influenced by his peer group.

I said I could prove that he was not correct, and he

accepted the challenge.

I then asked him how he had decided to grow the mustache above his upper lip.

"That's where it is *supposed to be*," he said. He was aware immediately that he had accepted an outside criterion. "I don't see where else I could have grown it," he added.

"You could have grown it on your right cheek in a circle," I said.

The issue here, at least to some people, is one of conformity, something other than tradition or conventionality, although these terms are often confused. In conformity, I believe a person essentially is agreeing to do something that he may or may not wish to do. He is doing it (deferring) so that he receives desired responses from others.

Tradition or conventionality involves an act which represents an established and prolonged process of the culture.

For example, businessmen in our society traditionally wear neckties. If an individual were "afraid" not to wear a tie on a particular occasion, then he could be perceived as conforming if he wore one.

To conform is to defer, so as to avoid the loss of the other person's positive responses.

As I have argued, young adults learn to conform as children. They defer to the demands of their parents, who are physically larger than they are. Later, as I have suggested, they may learn to be responsible for the feelings of other people. And, still later, they may begin conforming to a new parent (usually peer group). They are not "free." They are not the declaring adults who deal with issues and with data.

My experience has been that when young adults are asked to follow along this line of reasoning, they perceive it quickly and can modify their behavior to one in which they gather data and deal with issues.

The drug situation offers good examples.

A student one morning advised me that he had been smoking marijuana regularly.

"Why shouldn't I?" he asked. "Besides, you can't stop me." "Right," I replied, "but what might happen if you didn't smoke?"

"Well, I'd be missing out. Life wouldn't be so full of kicks. I'd probably have to get some new friends," he said.

I asked, "When you smoke grass or take some other drug, what is really happening?"

"Tell me," he said.

"I think what happens is that you are changing your nervous system, revising your perception of the world. And, one might hope, the change is temporary and reversible."

His response was not unusual. He said that he rather enjoyed getting away from the real world with all of its very real problems. But, he added, he also was glad to be able to return to the actual world.

Parenthetically, I have always been fascinated by the term, "drug trip." Even though a user can take only his own trip (within his own nervous system), he almost always desires that other people go tripping with him. The same socializing requirement is common with alcohol. Of course the difficulty usually increases in the person who doesn't need to socialize to do these things. Drinking alone, for example, is a strong symptomatic condition for alcoholism.

To the student, I said that I thought two things happen in a drug situation. First, the user experiences something that is real only to him. And, secondly, he probably is taking the drug on the basis of "ought to" or "supposed to."

After some thought, this student was able to agree with me.

My experience has been that young adults, given the opportunity, frequently have little real difficulty looking at this kind of situation in terms of issues and data rather than in terms of demonstrating their own independence. They usually can agree that drug activity is not appropriate or especially desirable since it leads nowhere except to a temporary escape from the real world, and often a deferring submission to peer pressure. They can perceive that they actually are meeting the real world with suffering, anger, or even helplessness and then attaching drug activity as an escape.

My contention has been that if we older adults were less open in our intense concern (usually expressed in "feelings") about some of the things younger people do, they probably would stop doing them sooner.

When I was young, drugs were available, including marijuana. My parents and the establishment and my peer group *agreed* that smoking pot was not something particularly desirable to do. In those days, we did not agree, however, on the desirability of smoking cigarettes and drinking beer. And those activities were apparently as distressing to parents then as doing drugs is to parents now, at least in the psychological implications.

What can parents do to help develop more effective relationships between themselves and their children, especially those still living at home?

I encourage parents to modify their typical behavior and instead of *demanding* more, to *declare* more. This may require some new learning on the part of parents.

I fully realize that parents cannot forgo responsibility for their teen-age son or daughter, and I'm not suggesting that they do. But I am suggesting that they demand less and negotiate more in more situations with the focus on issues and data rather than responsibility for feelings.

When a young person leaves home at about eighteen to enter college or to take a job, it is important that he has learned how to handle his relationships with other people so that he emerges as an effective "first-person-singular" individual, not someone who sings like whatever person he stands next to in the "choir."

Parents can speed this developing process by honing in on issues, by sharing data, and by negotiating.

At times, parents may still have to say no. It is essential that they understand, however, that when their young adult is at this age, he probably will not fulfill on demand what it is that they want to happen. Therefore, maintaining demands at low frequency will be more appropriate than the attempts at minute control that we so often witness in our society.

The traditional parental control tools in our culture are these, in chronological order:

* *I'm bigger than you are, so do what I say.*
* *Be responsible for my feelings, so do what I say.*

And when these fail, as they often do, there is typically a last ditch effort employing economic sanctions:

* *I control the money, so do what I say.*

In reality, when a child has grown as large or larger than his parents, they cannot literally make him do anything, even with the imposition of economic sanctions. For many parents, this is a difficult lesson to learn, but one that is true nevertheless.

A final point in this chapter.

The declarer always declares in the present, not in the past or in the future. The only time I am alive is right now, present tense.

Alan Watts once said that "history is a disease."

How often we play ancient history in a relationship, which wastes the here and now.

Emerson wrote:

> These roses under my window make no reference to former roses or to better ones; they are for what they are; they exist with God today. There is no time to them. There is simply the rose; it is perfect in every moment of its existence. Before a leaf-bud has burst, its whole life acts; in the full-blown flower there is no more; in the leafless root there is no less Its nature is satisfied and it satisfies nature in all moments alike. But man postpones or remembers; he does not live in the present, but with reverted eye laments the past, or, heedless of the riches that surround him, stands on tiptoe to foresee the future. He cannot be happy and strong until he too lives with nature in the present, above time.[1]

And Watts added:

> The past is not here except in the reflected form of memory. The future is not here except in the imagined form of anticipation. And as a consequence of that, one lives an impoverished present...because the

---

[1] Ralph Waldo Emerson, Essays (Boston and New York: Houghton Mifflin and Company, Cambridge, Mass.: The Riverside Press, 1883).

present is reduced to the hairline crosspoint that stands between the past which is gone and the future which is not yet here.[2]

The self-responsible declarer does not fret about the past nor is he anxious about the future. He is time-competent.

Does that mean that he lives only for today and with no thought of tomorrow?

Not at all.

He prepares for the future by being alive in the present.

If he wants to become a respected surgeon five years from now, he doesn't spend his present in fantasy. Instead, he does those things now that may lead to the position he seeks in five years.

From the Bible: "Be not anxious." To me that means, operationally: deal with the *now*. Behave in an appropriate and worthwhile way for you as a unique, unrepeatable, unprecedented human being.

---

[2] Trabscribed from Alan Watts: Divine Madness, #1010, produced by Big Sur Recordings, 2015 Bridgeway, Sausalito, Calif., 94065.

eight

A First-Person Singular Freedom

Summary

And there you have it.

If you have been a Flat Earth person, you may wish to try looking at your world of relationships from this new Round Earth perspective. At least I hope so. I hope you have stopped bumping along enough to experience what freedom I think can be yours.

Okayness concerns your *present* behavior and whether that behavior is appropriate and worthwhile for you. Are your transactions with other people as worthwhile and as appropriate as you'd like them to be?

Here in brief is what I have been suggesting:

> Each of us learns to do what we do, how to behave in interpersonal relationships. What was learned from parents and others in authority can be modified by new learning; new ways of behaving can be added.
>
> In behaving, we seek to have happen what we want to happen. When we are blocked from getting what we want

to happen, most of us have learned to use the get-my-way tools of helplessness, suffering, and anger. When that occurs, we are asking other people to be responsible for our feelings.

Words present us with great difficulty in relationships because they often represent abstractions rather than happenings or events. We internalize them so much that they become nearly realities in themselves.

When we use a more operational language, we describe what is actually happening or what we wish to happen.

Most people have learned three ways of behaving in interpersonal transactions: deferring, demanding, and defecting. All three are designed to win but are destined to lose.

A fourth option exists, but most people are unaware of it. This new alternative, or language, is to declare, in the first person singular, what one wants to happen in operational terms, inviting the partner to do so also. This leads to self-responsibility rather than other-responsibility. I am responsible for my behavior by being responsive to the situation I share with others.

Through years of presenting the ideas in this book to other people, I have encountered the occasional person who responds that my approach to human relationships is uncaring and cold. I do not think so. The issue is one of control vs. concern.

Being under the control of another person or working to control him through feelings does not lead to personal freedom or appropriate behavior, in my opinion.

I can be *concerned* about another person by being aware of him, and by being *responsive* to the situation in which we are relating.

I was reading Allen Wheelis just the other day. In *How People Change* (New York, Harper & Row, 1973), Wheelis writes: "Since we are what we do, if we want to change what we are we must begin by changing what we do, must undertake a new mode of action."

Later, he explains: "If, however, one's destiny is shaped from within then one has become more of a creator, has gained freedom."

To me, the declarer is the most creative person in our society, a person whose creativity invites him to attain a freedom he once may have thought impossible.

He has a first-person-singular freedom, a first-person-singular worthwhileness.

Suggested Additional Readings

Breggin, Peter R., *Toxic Psychiatry* (St. Martin's Press, 1991)

Leo, John, "Doing the Disorder Rag" (U.S. News and World Report, October 27, 1997, page 20)

Papanicolaou, A.C., Emotion: *A Reconsideration of the Somatic Theory* (Gordon and Breach Science Publishers, 1988)

Piattelli-Palmarini, Massimo, *Inevitable Illusions* (John Wiley and Sins, Inc., 1994)

Szasz, Thomas, *The Myth of Psychotherapy* (Syracuse University Press, 1988)

index

notes